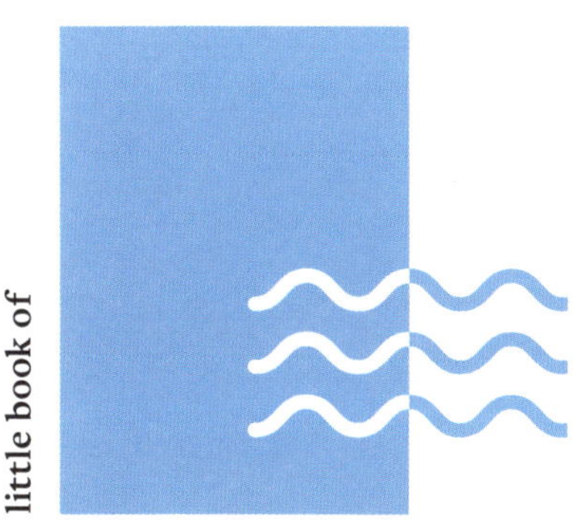

COPENHAGEN style

Published in 2025 by Welbeck
An Imprint of HEADLINE PUBLISHING GROUP LIMITED

1

Cataloguing in Publication Data is available from the British Library

ISBN 9781035425266

Printed in China

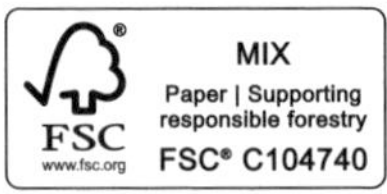

Headline's policy is to use papers that are natural, renewable and recyclable products and made from wood grown in well-managed forests and other controlled sources. The logging and manufacturing processes are expected to conform to the environmental regulations of the country of origin.

HEADLINE PUBLISHING GROUP LIMITED
An Hachette UK Company
Carmelite House
50 Victoria Embankment
London EC4Y 0DZ

The authorised representative in the EEA is Hachette Ireland, 8 Castlecourt Centre, Dublin 15, D15 XTP3, Ireland (email: info@hbgi.ie)

www.headline.co.uk
www.hachette.co.uk

GLENYS JOHNSON

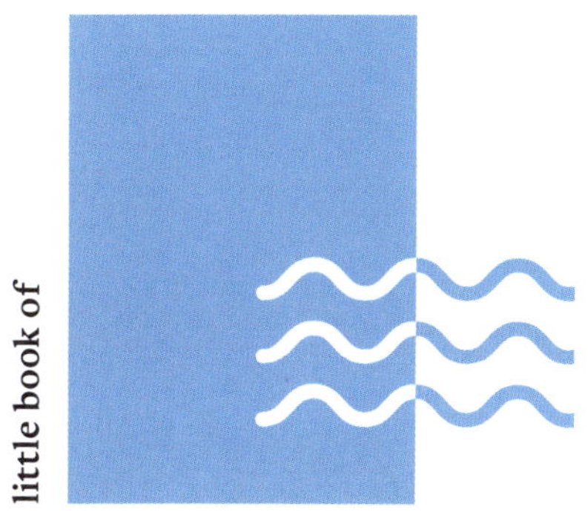

COPENHAGEN style

The Fashion Story of the Iconic City

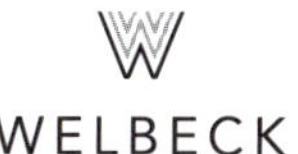
WELBECK

CONTENTS

chapter 1

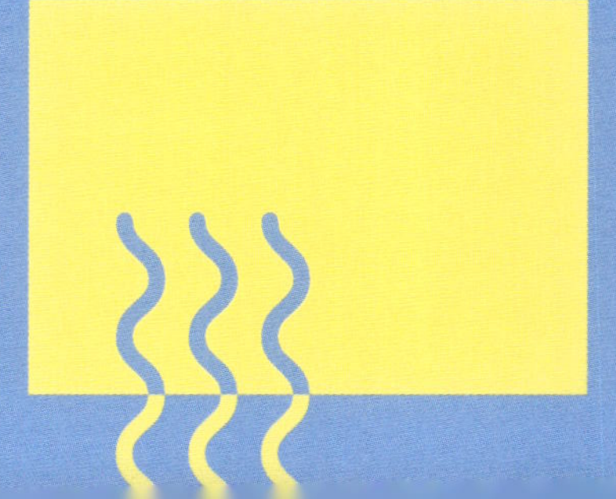

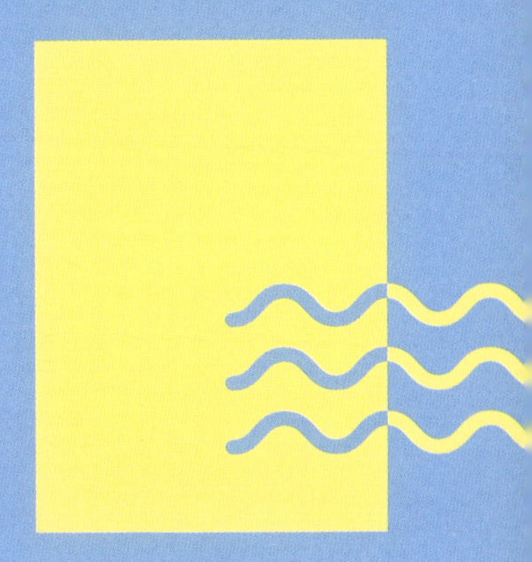

THE CITY'S ROOTS

What is now often credited with being one of the world's most fashionable cities has a history that isn't dissimilar to many other European ports. Due to its geographical location on the Øresund strait, the area was a prime location for the site of a Viking fishing village which is said to have been established in the eleventh century. Since then, the city's focus on culture, education and urban modernization, including projects like the Øresund Bridge, ensured its relevance and growth as a dynamic Scandinavian capital.

The climate of the city is characterized by cool temperatures and plenty of rainfall for much of the year, with summers being mild (yet warm enough for the Danes to enjoy frequent swims in the sea). This sometimes challenging forecast has helped shape the wardrobe associated with Copenhagen residents and their dedication to balancing practicality with aesthetic appeal. Knitwear styles, practical footwear that's ready to take on the ice and puddles, and waterproof outerwear and jeans that allow for comfortable cycling across the city throughout the year have played a key role in shaping the city's style. The famous Danish carefree attitude is often expressed through the apparel of Copenhageners: the city's residents look to casual cuts and playful colour palettes and prints.

Hand-drawn poster depicting Copenhagen, Denmark.

COPENHAGEN
DENMARK

FOLK CLOTHING

One of the first mentions of Danish national dress is reported to be from 1788 when a public essay competition asked: "Is it useful or advantageous to introduce a national dress?" The response to this was mixed but many stated that this would be restrictive to Danes and therefore should be rejected, though it was agreed that government officials should sport some kind of uniform to identify themselves. By the mid-1800s, Denmark was shifting further toward the notion of an official uniform being developed to promote the visual identity of Danes. In order to define what exactly this would be, the Danish National Museum commissioned a painter by the name of F.C. Lund to travel across the country to paint Danes in their daily lives to document the styles that were being worn.

This series of paintings depicted a range of styles crafted mainly from natural fibres including wool, linen and cotton, primarily designed for warmth in the cooler climate. These styles included skirts (*nederdel*), a blouse (*skjorte*) with intricate embroidery or lace details, an apron and a bonnet or scarf to cover the hair. Men's attire included knitted sweaters (*trøje*) and woollen trousers. The women's bonnet was a very popular accessory of the period and was also used as a key tool in communicating the marital status, class and region of the wearer. Many daughters of craftsmen were said to have engaged in the art of making bonnets and would pass on the skill to their daughters and granddaughters to carry on the tradition. Clogs (*træsko*) were also a key piece in the wardrobes of both men and women of varying regions and

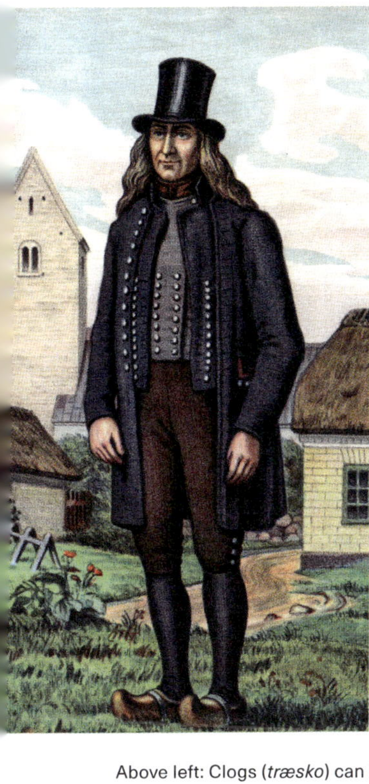

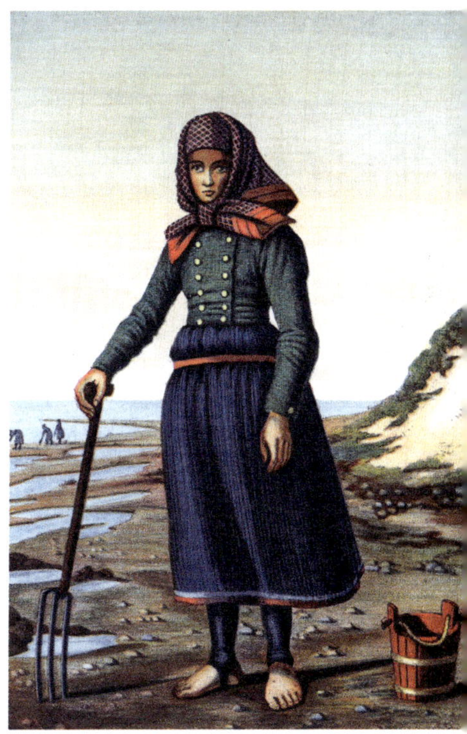

Above left: Clogs (*træsko*) can be seen on the feet of this painting by F.C. Lund which presents a man referred to as "the fur man".

Above right: Referred to simply as "girl from Baavand", F.C. Lund's depiction of this Danish woman shows one of the common styles of dress for the mid-nineteenth century.

social classes. The wooden footwear style in Denmark can be traced back as early as the fifteenth century. Renowned Danish storyteller Hans Christian Andersen confirms the popularity of clogs in Danish society by mentioning the footwear style in many of his stories.

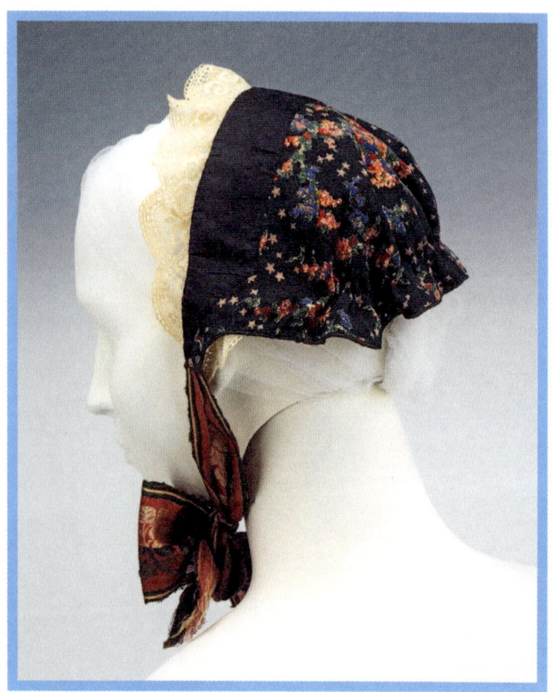

Now housed at the Metropolitan Museum of Art in New York City, this bonnet is said to have belonged to an unmarried woman from the Danish island of Lolland.

Folk dancers in Denmark continue to sport these traditional styles with pride while some contemporary Danish fashion designers like Cecilie Bahnsen and Henrik Vibskov have also looked to the country's folk dress for inspiration. Like many aspects of Danish society, clothing styles evolved with trends and technologies over the years. As Copenhagen became a more established trading site through the nineteenth century, apparel styles would be diversified and democratized to new heights.

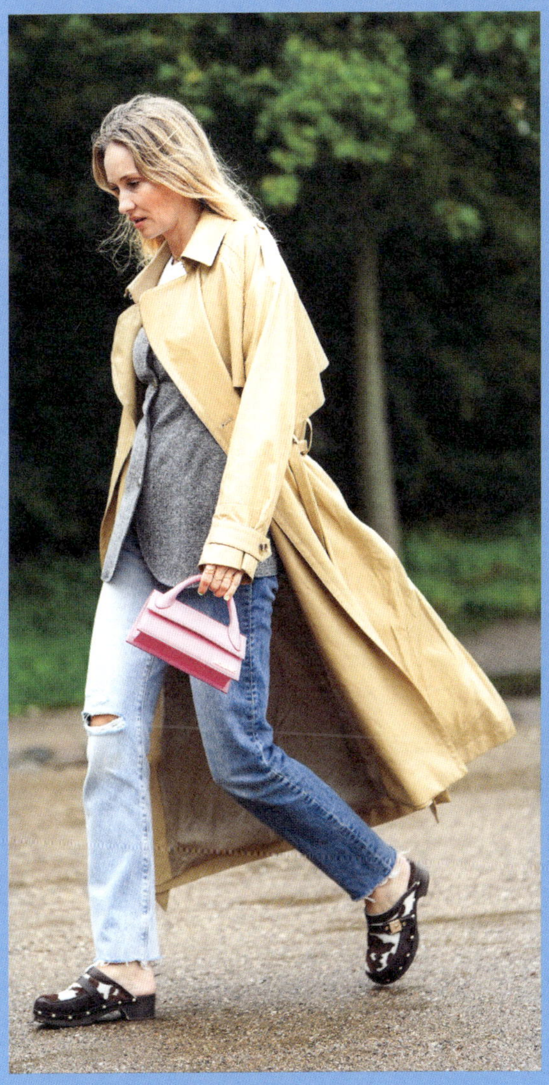

A 2024 Copenhagen Fashion week attendee accessorizes with a pink handbag from Jacquemus and cow print mules.

DENMARK'S FIRST FASHION QUEEN

One of Copenhagen's young residents through this pivotal period, born in December 1844 as Alexandra Caroline Marie Charlotte Louise Julia, would soon become one of the first key players in establishing the city as a subject for fashion lovers around the world.

Growing up in a relatively modest home for someone who would go on to become a globally respected royal, Queen Alexandra of Denmark is said to have experienced a happy childhood where the legendary Hans Christian Andersen himself shared magical stories with her and her siblings. But her life would change quite dramatically when her father, a Danish army general, found himself heir to the throne in 1852. This shift made Alexandra a hot topic for other royal families across Europe and would eventually lead to the Crown Princess Victoria of Prussia setting her up with the then-young bachelor that was Albert Edward, the Prince of Wales. It wouldn't be long before she found herself with the new title of Princess of Wales and a new address in the United Kingdom.

Alexandra of Denmark (1844–1925) was known for her choker-style necklaces that she used to hide a scar on her neck.

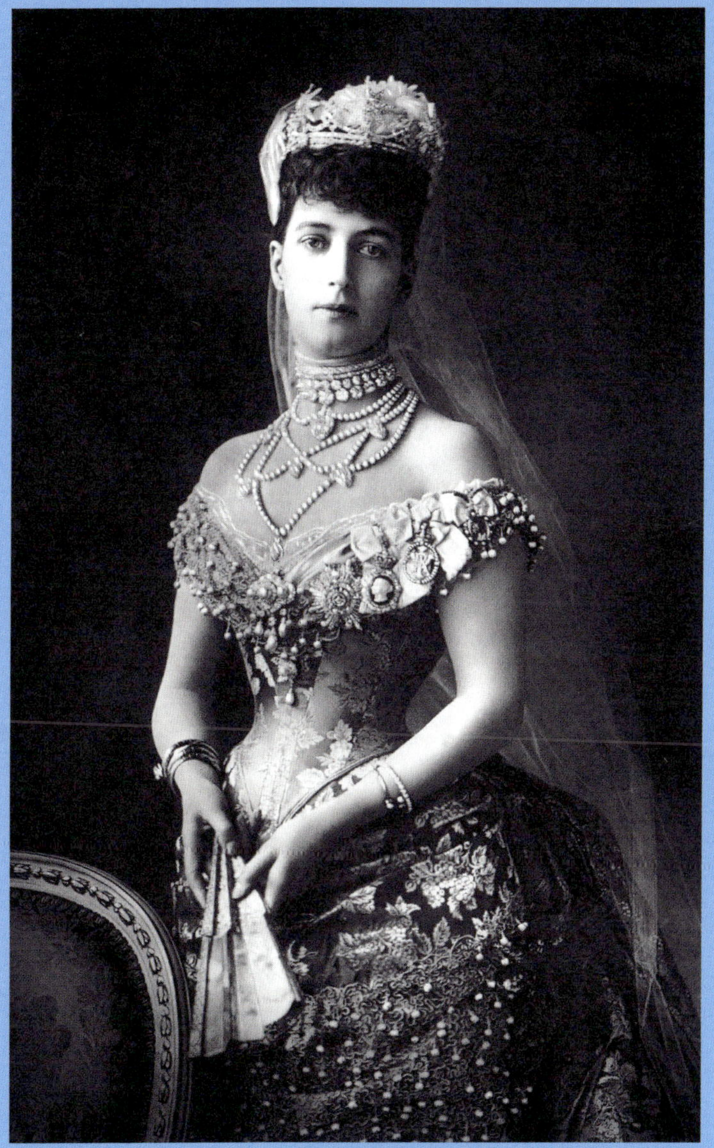

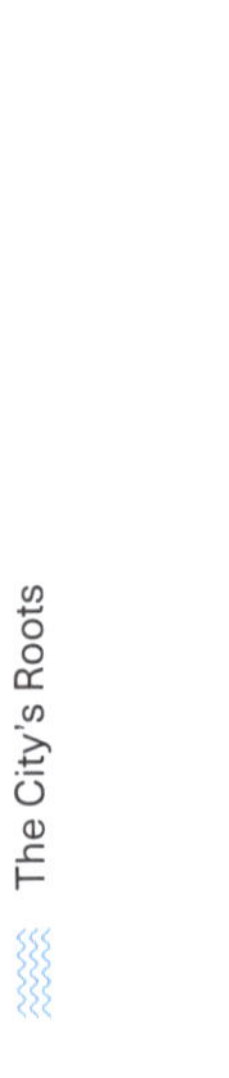

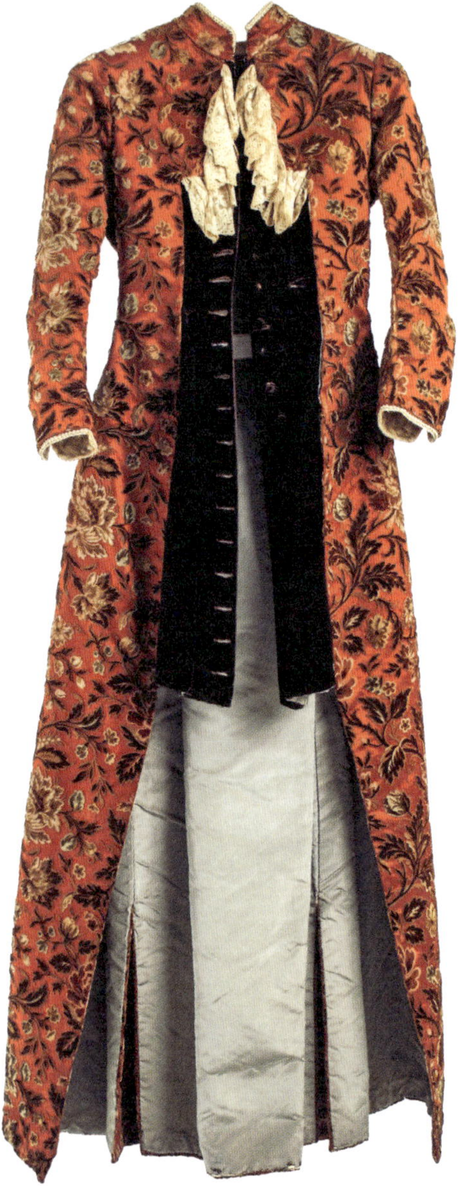

Queen Alexandra would become an influential character regarding women's fashion at the time. One of her more notable styles was a selection of chokers and high-necked gowns which the Dane adopted to conceal a scar she acquired following surgery she underwent as a child. Elly Summers, the curator behind the exhibition *Royal Women* at the Museum of Fashion in Bath, told the BBC: "She was a fashion icon and people would copy what she was wearing [...] She forged her own look, she was very involved in crafting her image, and she was a trend setter, even if it wasn't necessarily on purpose."

By the 1870s, Alexandra had adopted a tailored two-piece outfit as her signature style, playing a role in establishing the corset-style top and skirt combo as a must-have style for many women of the era. Queen Alexandra's influence on the fashion world has inspired various exhibitions across the globe including *Color Through the Decades & Costumes and Accessories Worn by Queen Alexandra of England* in 1941 at the Museum of Costume Art, now the Costume Institute at the Metropolitan Museum of Art.

Designed by M.A. Connelly, this suiting style from Queen Alexandra's wardrobe is indicative of her preference for a two-piece ensemble.

THE SHOPPING SCENE

As the Danish royals were setting trends, the everyday Dane was also becoming more interested in fashionable apparel. In 1870, Magasin du Nord opened its first retail space in Hotel du Nord on the King's New Square (*Kongens Nytorv*) in the city centre. By the turn of the twentieth century, the now iconic retailer had expanded significantly and moved into its flagship store, built in place of the Hotel du Nord, which was demolished in 1893. The arrival of Magasin du Nord and other retailers like Daells Varehus (1910) and Illum (1891) moved the city's residents away from relying on traditional tailoring or homemade clothing and towards ready-to-wear fashion. The success of this new way to shop was evident in the Magasin du Nord franchise that grew from 50 branches in 1892 to 98 by 1906.

The arrival of these new spaces would also play a key role in promoting trends from abroad among Copenhagen shoppers and encouraging fashion-focused locals to add their own twists to looks from further afield. The introduction of department stores in Copenhagen also drew new energy into the city, with many hosting events and using their windows as an opportunity to showcase apparel in a new way that older methods – like catalogues – couldn't offer. Magasin du Nord's "exhibits" would attract both tourists and locals alike for their extravagant displays with press reportedly comparing them to "an Aladdin's castle". This shift towards shopping becoming a preferred pastime for many Danes and clothing being increasingly democratized would continue to grow through the coming years, establishing the city as a key destination for fashion lovers across the globe.

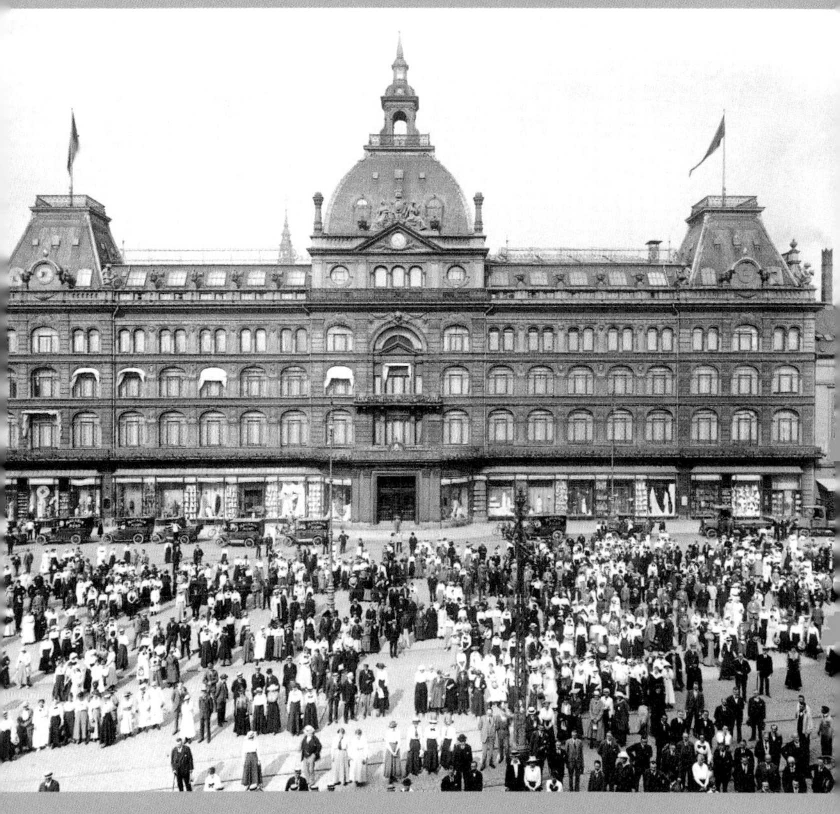

Above: To celebrate the retailer's 50th anniversary, Magasin du Nord's staff gather for a photo outside the Kongens Nytorv location in 1918.

Overleaf: Magasin du Nord's dress department has been a key source of inspiration for many Danish women, pictured here in 1918.

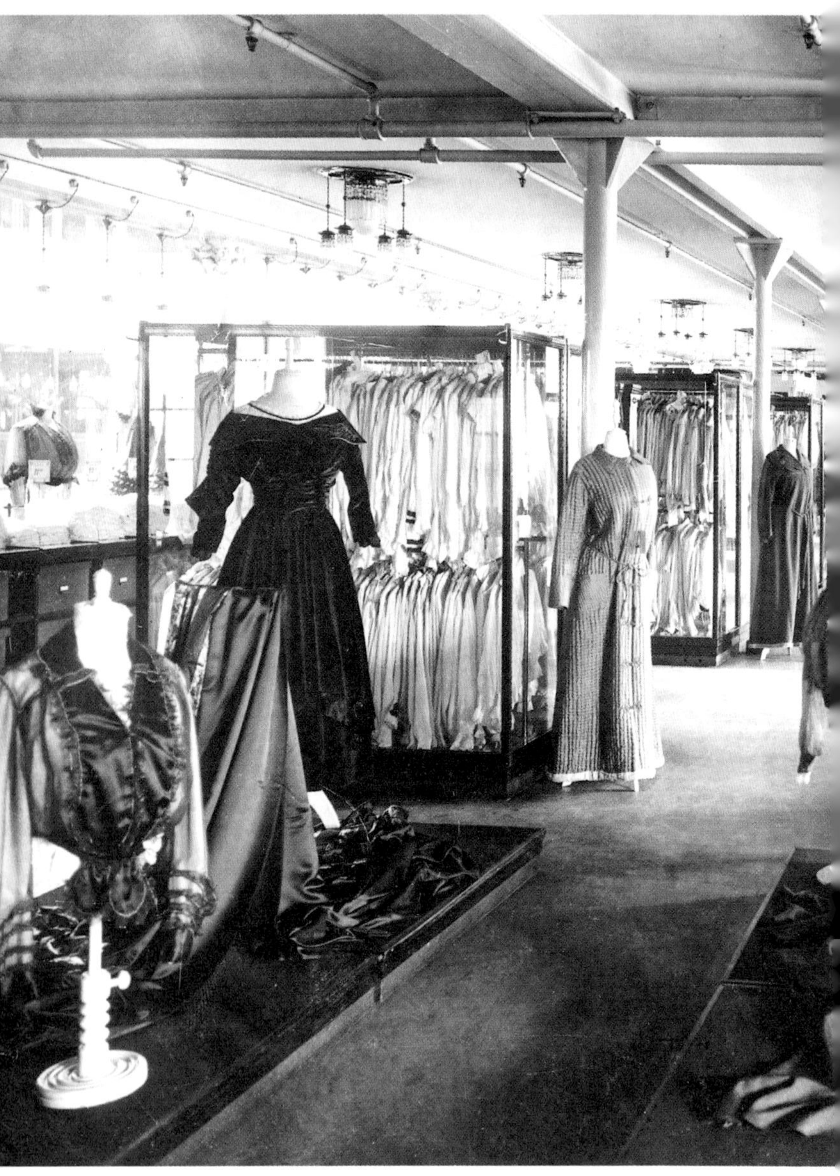

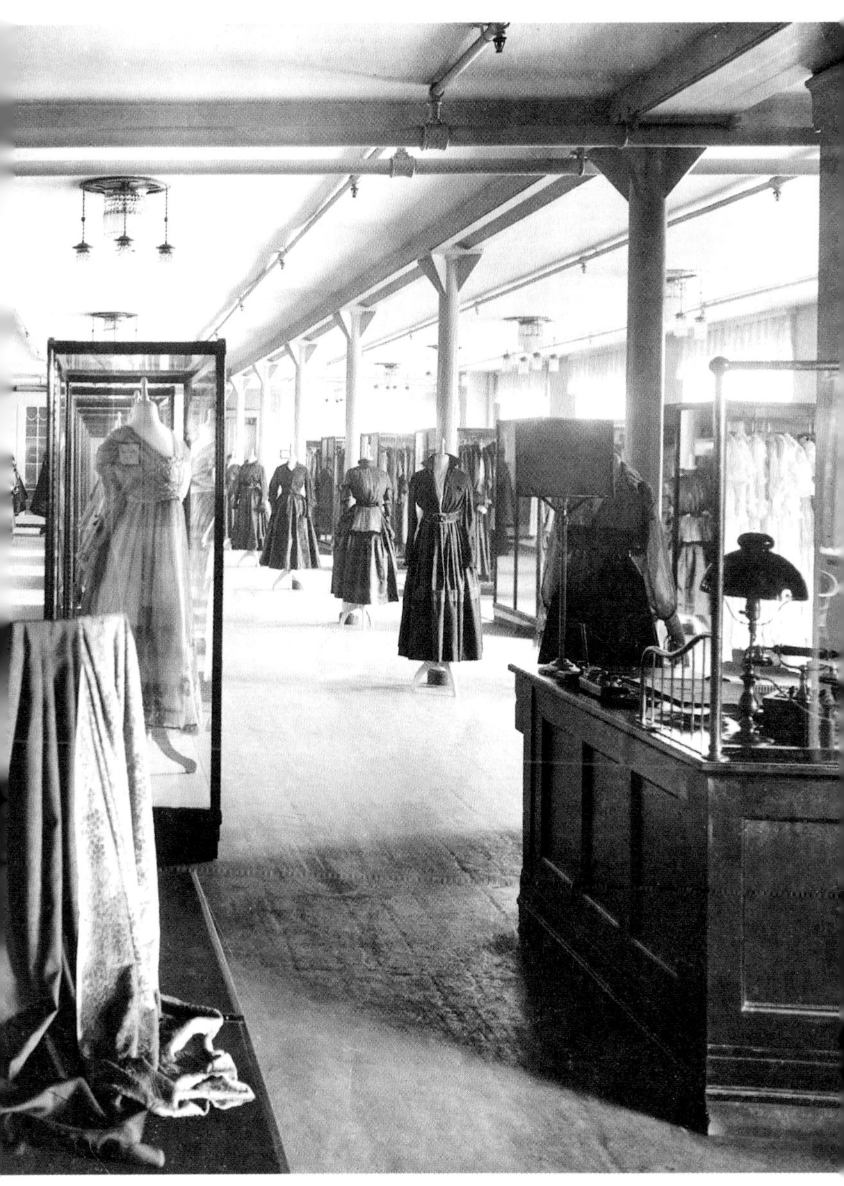

chapter 2

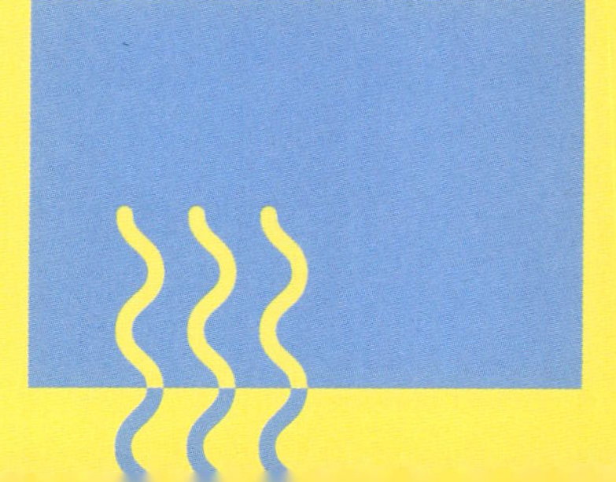

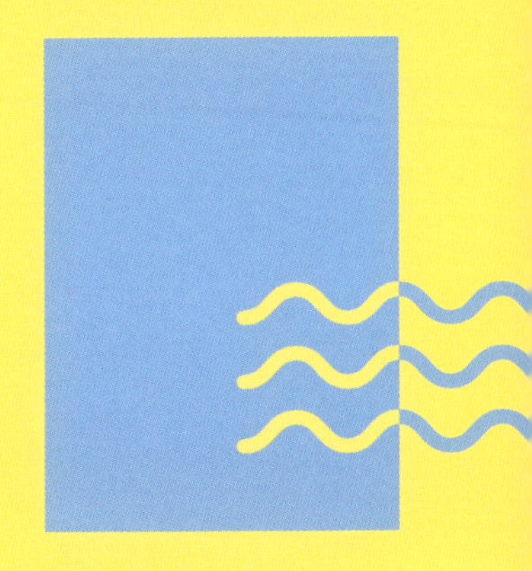

MiD-CENTURY MOOD

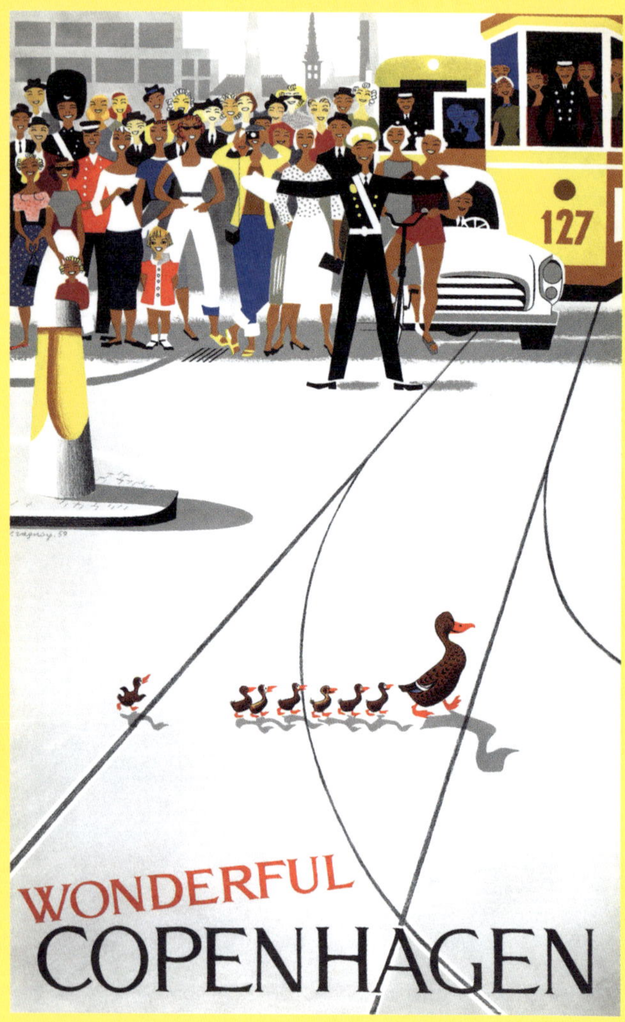

This Viggo Vagnby poster is rumoured to have been inspired by a true event that was featured in the Copenhagen press when a police officer stopped traffic for a family of ducks to cross a busy main road. The poster was used by the Tourist Association of Copenhagen throughout the 1950s.

In 1929, several countries across the globe experienced the start of what is now referred to as the Great Depression, a period where resources were scarce across nearly all industries and daily life became a serious struggle for many. This would encourage people to think differently, with a stark shift away from things viewed as frivolous. This mindset would also impact design, particularly in the world of architecture. The new preferred style that grew out of this approach would be referred to across the Nordic countries as simply *Funkis*.

Often referred to as an architectural and design philosophy that prioritizes practicality and simplicity over ornate decoration, Funkis gained momentum across Scandinavia notably after the Stockholm Exhibition in 1930 where it was introduced to the general public as a new vision of modern living that emphasized standardization in housing. The Lagkagehuset building on Christianshavns Torv designed by Edvard Thomsen, and Arne Jacobsen's Bellevue, Bellavista and Bellevue Theatre are key designs that embody Funkis style.

As functionality became a prime focus for the city's architecture, the shift in other areas of design was also becoming apparent. Alongside architecture and furniture design, Danish fashion developed a reputation both locally and abroad during the mid-twentieth century, helping pave the way for notable labels and designers. This would lead to Danish design across different disciplines being cemented as a coveted style across the globe for decades to come.

Overleaf: Located in Klampenborg, just north of Copenhagen, Arne Jacobsen's Bellavista housing estate is one of the country's most popular examples of the Funkis style.

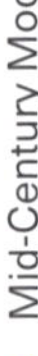

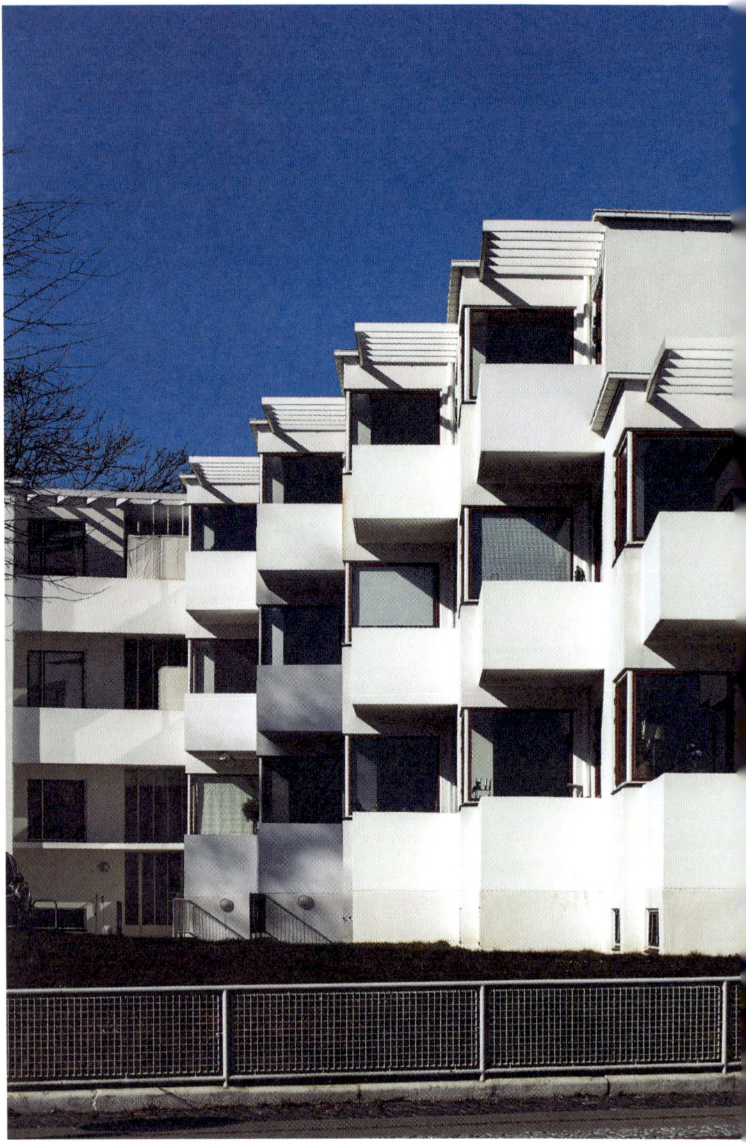

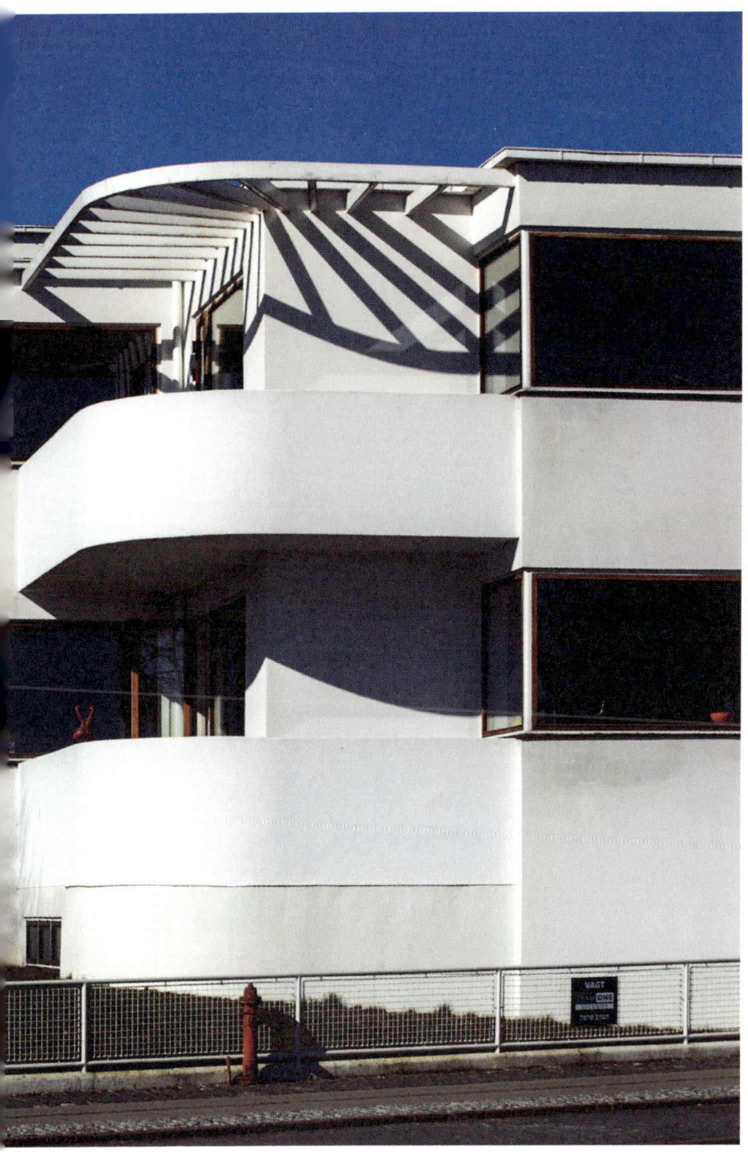
VAGT

DANISH MODERN IS BORN

Following the Second World War, it's said that Denmark experienced a new era regarding the identity of Danish fashion. There was a change in clothing being designed and produced in Denmark by Danish designers. By this time, Danish Modern had gathered traction internationally as a furniture design style known for its emphasis on functionality, simplicity and craftsmanship.

The Danish Modern movement was led by architect and furniture designer Kaare Klint, who pioneered a move away from the ornamental design philosophy that had previously been the primary aesthetic in many Western homes and encouraged more minimalist practices. As Design Museum Denmark puts it, "Modernists viewed the era's crowded living rooms with heavy furniture, velvet curtains, carpets, plants and an abundance of knick-knacks as an example of everything wrong with design and decoration. Danish Modern thus became their rebellion against the 'style confusion' they believed prevailed until the 1920s." Klint inspired some of the leading designers of the time including Hans J. Wegner, Arne Jacobsen, Finn Juhl and Verner Panton.

This fresh take on design quickly spread across the globe with names like Dansk Designs becoming a hit in many American homes throughout the mid-twentieth century. Some of Copenhagen's most popular sites were filled with the work of some of these design icons: Copenhagen's Radisson Collection Royal Hotel (formally SAS Royal Hotel) was designed by Arne Jacobsen, creator of the iconic Egg Chair, a piece still perennially popular to this day.

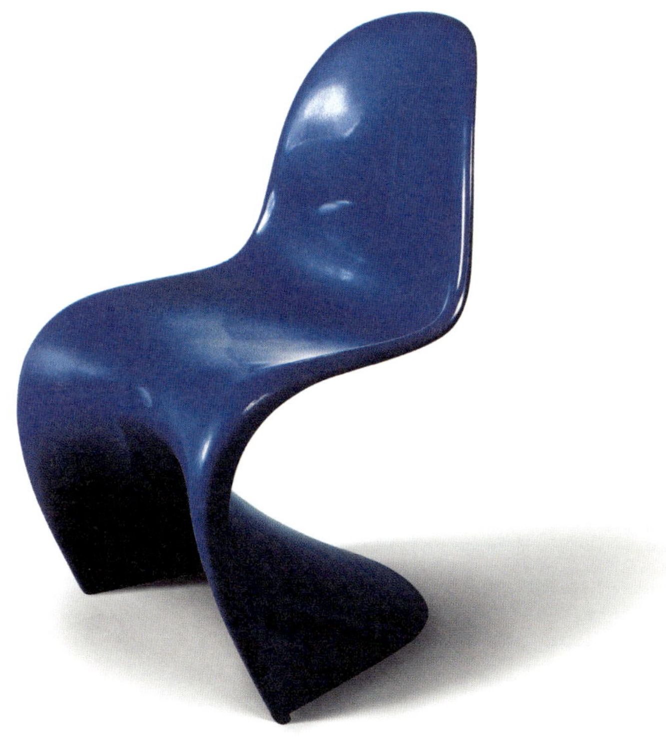

The Panton Chair was designed by Verner Panton in 1958 and is a Danish design classic.

Some believe that the design philosophy that these visionaries helped form, through their timeless yet innovative approaches, would influence fashion designers of the period. However, it's important to note that others at the time would quickly highlight that those in fashion and many Danish Modern furniture designers held opposing views – with the former focused on generating revenue and the latter focused on socialism and creating items that promoted living a "good life".

COUTURE COMES TO COPENHAGEN

Until the early to mid-twentieth century, retailers like Magasin du Nord, Illum and Daells Varehus were responsible for dressing much of the Danish capital's fashion-forward residents – focusing on international designs, and like many other Western cosmopolitan cities, French couture was among the most coveted. A group which many refer to as "The three big Bs" would do wonders for bringing couture to Copenhagen: Holger Blom, Uffe Brydegaard and Preben Birch.

Brydegaard and Birch made names for themselves by creating the costumes behind some of the period's most famous films, including *En ganske almindelig pige* starring Didder Rønlund and Kispus, noted as the first Danish film to be shot in colour. The two would both open their own boutiques in the city centre, catering to Copenhagen residents who desired the high fashion looks of their Parisian neighbours. But it was Blom that would do the most for the Danish public in the way of couture. Blom's career began by sewing dresses for private clients alongside his studies before dropping out and opening a shop of his own in 1930. Bodil Kjer, Liva Weel, Marguerite Viby and Helle Virkner were just some of his high-profile clients around that time. By the 60s, Blom's designs had become so coveted that Princess Anne-Marie went to the designer for a dress to wear when marrying Constantine II of Greece in Athens in 1964. The dress featured a rounded neckline, empire-line waist, full skirt and 18-foot train. The vast scale of the wedding led the Royal Central website to speculate that the dress could be one of the most famous of the twentieth century.

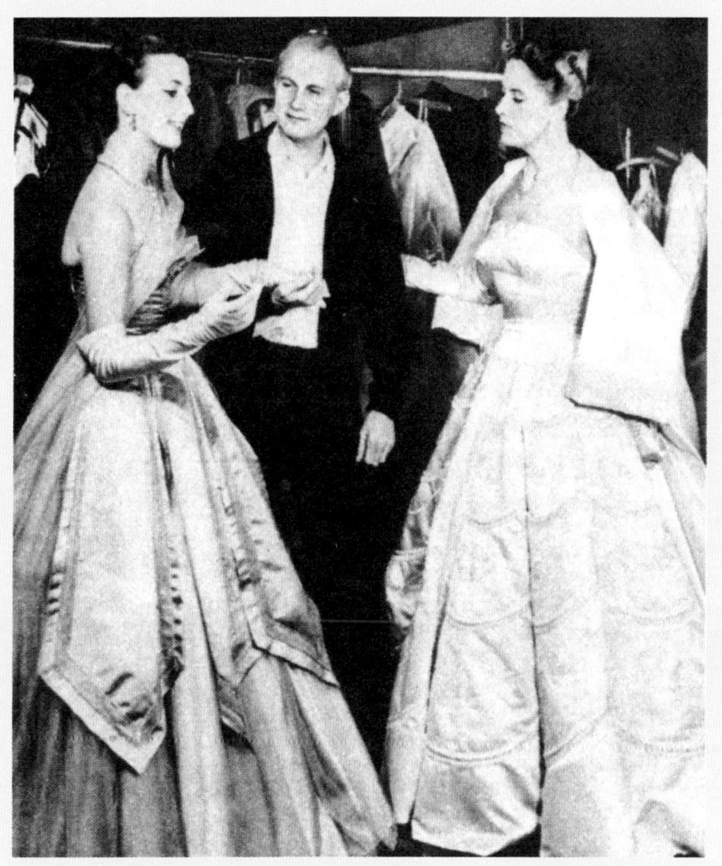

Designer Holger Blom with models sporting his couture designs, 1950.

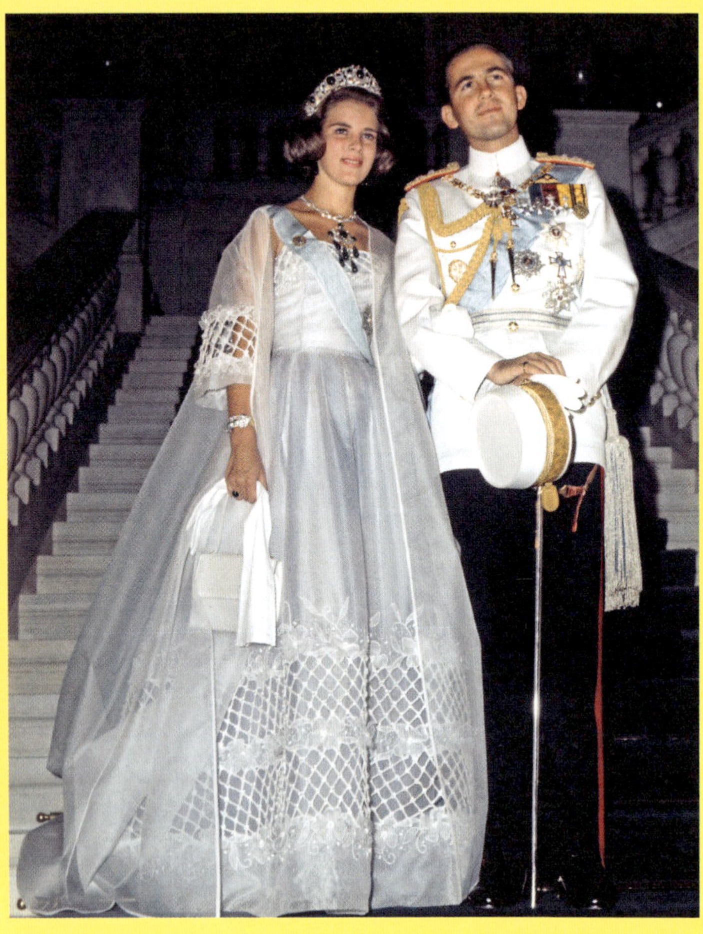

Princess Anne-Marie of Denmark wore a dress designed by Danish designer Holger Blom for her wedding to King Constantine II of Greece on 18 September 1964.

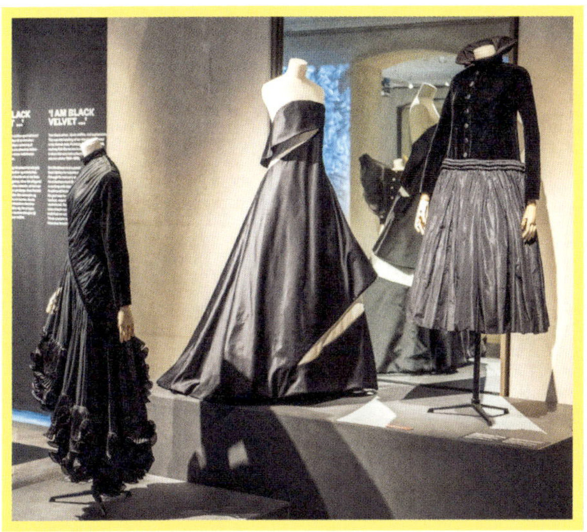

In 2017, Copenhagen's Museum of Design launched *I am Black Velvet*, an exhibition dedicated to the designs of Erik Mortensen and his contributions to the world of haute couture.

Though Blom would pass away in 1963, his legacy would live on – most notably through one of his apprentices, Erik Mortensen. A young Mortensen set his sights on working for Blom at an early age, moving from his hometown of Frederikshavn to Copenhagen to work for the iconic designer at just 16. By 22, Mortensen was off to Paris to work under Pierre Balmain. The young Dane would successfully work for Balmain and climb the ranks, eventually landing the role of head designer after Pierre's death in 1982. Mortensen went on to win a number of prestigious fashion awards, including the Dé d'Or, and design 17 collections while at Balmain. Though much of Mortensen's career took place in Paris, the designer's Danish roots helped to show the fashion industry that the Danes weren't to be underestimated.

A NEW ENERGY IN TOWN

Outside of the design world, Copenhagen was becoming a destination for another group in the mid-twentieth century – jazz lovers. It's reported that as early as the 1930s, jazz musicians from across the world were heading to the Danish capital. Many of these people were African American, noting that the atmosphere in Denmark was a lot kinder towards Black people during this time than what they experienced in America. In the 1940s, jazz was forced underground due to the Nazi occupation. By the mid-1960s, jazz was thriving in the city, as Copenhagen boasted a long list of jazz musicians like Dexter Gordon and Kenny Drew who would often play at Jazzhus Montmartre. This scene helped Copenhagen strengthen its reputation as an open society with a strong appreciation for the arts, encouraging creativity for both residents and visitors alike.

As the free-spirited jazz movement was filling smoke-filled bars across the city, Copenhagen would also experience a shift in attitudes towards another topic: sex. The Danes' liberal philosophy toward sex is deeply ingrained in the culture, something many attribute to the nineteenth-century pastor and poet Nikolaj Frederik Severin Grundtvig. He promoted the idea that one should be open to others' points of view, even if they don't align with your own – an idea that had a clear influence on Danish society. This viewpoint passed the test of time, and in 1969, Denmark made history by being the first country to legalize pornography. Though neighbouring Sweden had already gained an international reputation for its sexual cinematic outputs, this new law allowed Denmark to quickly gain traction in the field.

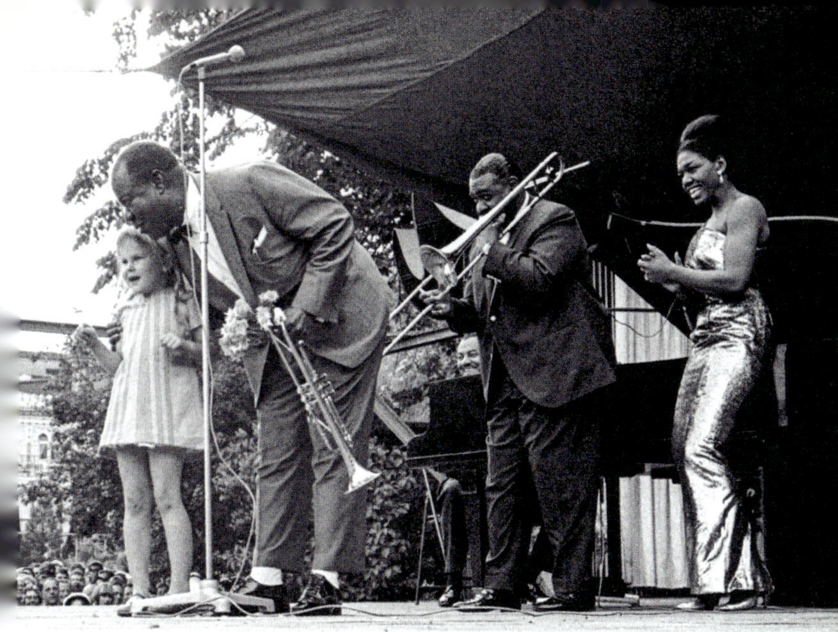

The iconic Louis Armstrong, seen here on stage in 1965, was just one of the many jazz musicians to perform at Copenhagen's Tivoli Gardens.

In a 1970 piece in *The New York Times*, American journalist Tom Buckley weighed in on pornography diversifying the Danish export trade, stating that it "will never rank with porcelain, silver ware, furniture, dairy products or hams and bacon as a prestige item, but several Danes I talked to noted slyly that the unblushing exertions of their young men and women were helping to offset a persistent trade deficit. 'That's what I call progress,' a Danish journalist said, repeating a quip that was making the rounds. 'From blue cheese to blue movies.'"

In 1971, another key occurrence in establishing Copenhagen's countercultural stance would occur – the establishment of Freetown Christiania. Starting as a military space taken over by squatters, the area was initially claimed by a group of

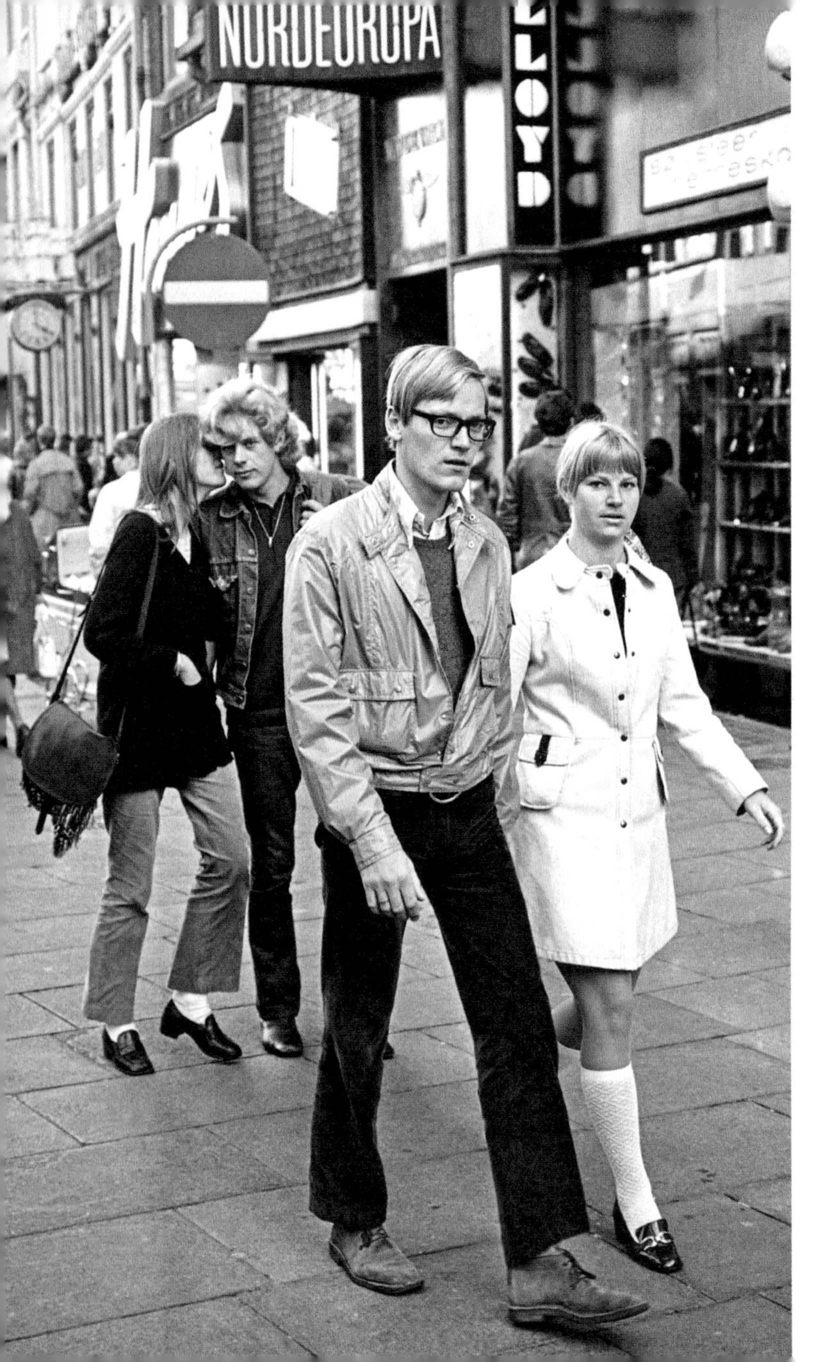
LLOYD

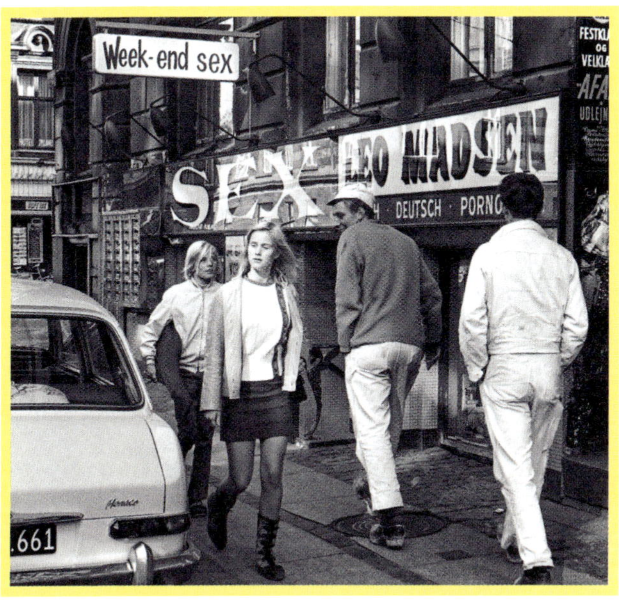

Opposite: Young Copenhagen locals stroll through the streets of the Danish capital, 1969.

Above: Copenhagen residents pass by one of the city's popular porn shops of the era, Leo Madsen, 1969.

about 50 individuals who were dissatisfied with the housing situation in Copenhagen at the time. Some were associated with the alternative local publication, *Hovedbladet*. This new, self-governing community attracted visitors from across Europe who wanted to witness the free-natured way of living centred around a community spirit that was free from all private cars and weapons. With this new settlement, the energy in Copenhagen was very much shifting, allowing the capital to solidify itself as one of the most open-minded cities in Europe at the time.

THE FRESH ERA OF FASHION

"The Danish clothing industry was transforming into a fashion industry, and this transformation took place in Copenhagen. Fashion gave the otherwise rundown city a lively kick, lending it the youthful energy of an industry eager to succeed as an international export powerhouse with a home base in Copenhagen."
Katrina Sark, *Copenhagen Chic*

With the energy of Copenhagen shifting, the clothing choices of its residents would need to keep up. By the 1970s, the fashion shows of the city's top fashion retailers had dissipated as the demand changed towards more casual, youthful fashions. This could partially be credited to the phenomenon of the "teenager", which many agree to be inspired by the United States. Several Copenhagen-based department stores are said to have dedicated portions of their retail space and marketing towards this new consumer demographic while boutiques dedicated to "youth fashion" began to spring up across the city centre. Names like Nørgaard på Strøget and Deres had become the go-to spots for those looking to adopt the more modern looks of the time.

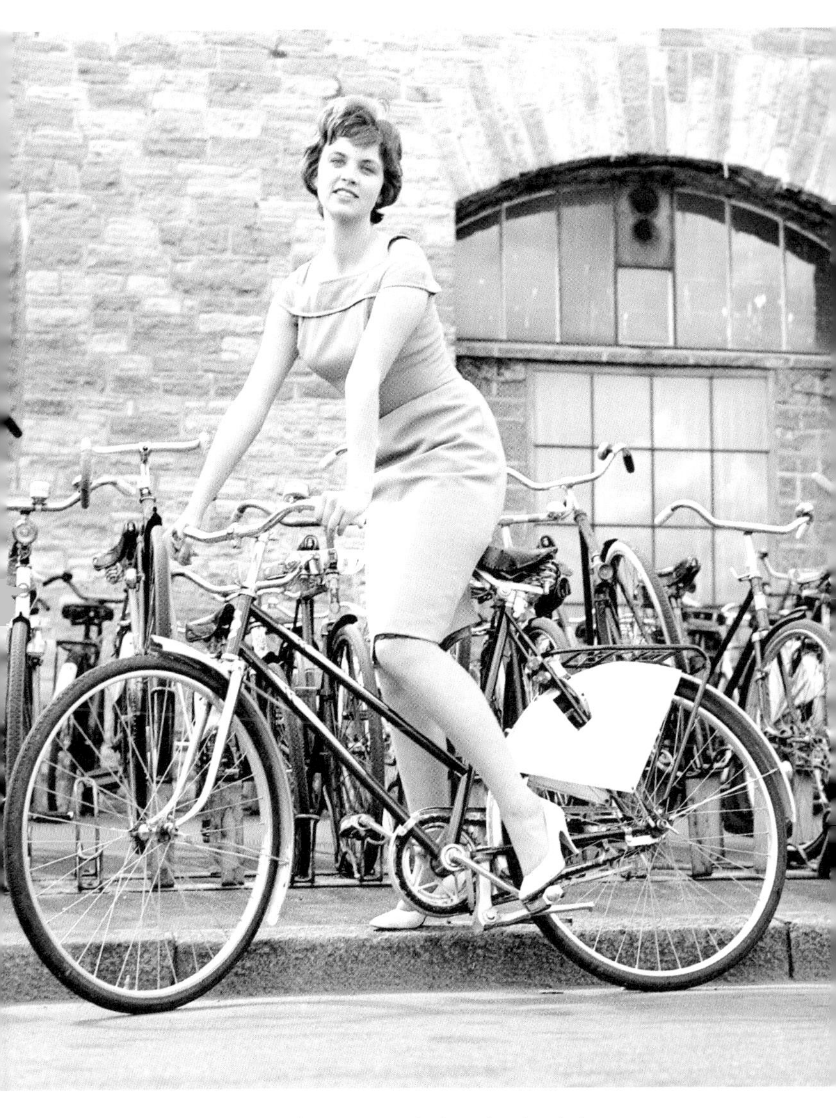

Local woman demonstrates the love that the city's residents have for the bicycle, 1960.

“Danish fashion emerged [...] and the export adventures of youth fashion brands appeared in newspaper headlines at home and abroad; this highlighted the independence of Danish fashion, no longer a copy of international fashion, but something new and independent.”
Marie Riegels Melchior

In the 1970s, a new group of designers were emerging in the Danish capital and promoting Danish fashion with their playful and bohemian looks. Looking at this period, renowned fashion journalist Lotte Freddie shared her musings in a 2008 interview: “Margit Brandt and Dranella were the first ones. Dranella came first and then Margit, it was something completely new, which was defiantly design.”

Margit Brandt’s career began after she graduated from Copenhagen’s Margrethe-Skolen (now known as the Scandinavian Academy of Fashion Design), before going to Paris to apprentice for names like Balmain. She would go on to launch the label B-age with her husband Erik Brandt at the Copenhagen Fashion Fair in 1965. The couple’s jet-setting lifestyle would see them become friends with some of the hottest celebrities at the time (notably Mick Jagger, Andy Warhol and David Bowie). The couple’s designs would be likened to the UK’s Mary Quant and sold across the world in their shops in the USA, Switzerland, Japan and Hong Kong. Undoubtedly one of Denmark’s most respected names in fashion, Brandt’s designs and legacy continue to be recognized by the Danish fashion industry today.

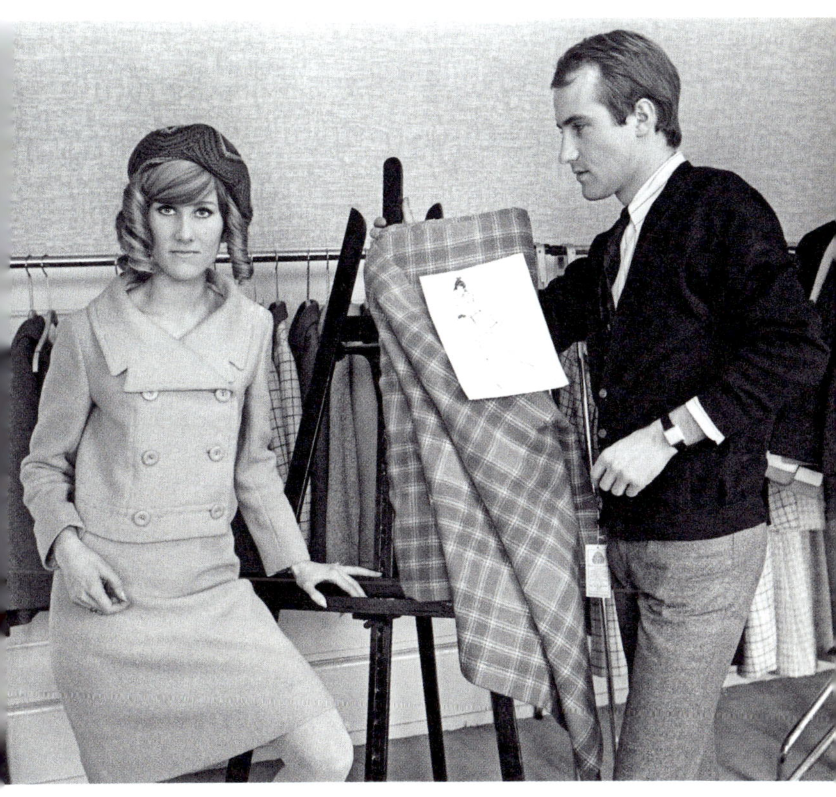

Above: Pictured here in 1966, Danish designer couple Margit and Erik Brandt played a key role in attracting attention to Danish fashion design.

Overleaf: Margit Brandt's reach was evident by her designs appearing in international fashion publications, like this 1969 edition of *Vogue*.

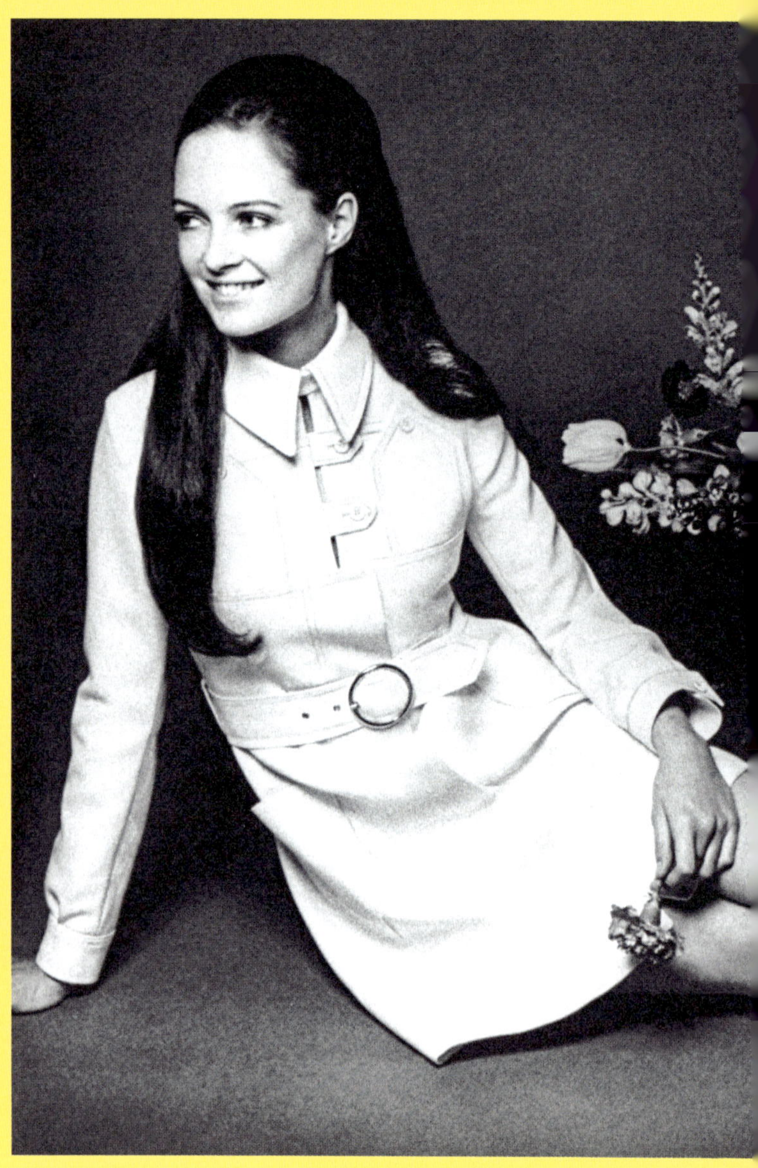

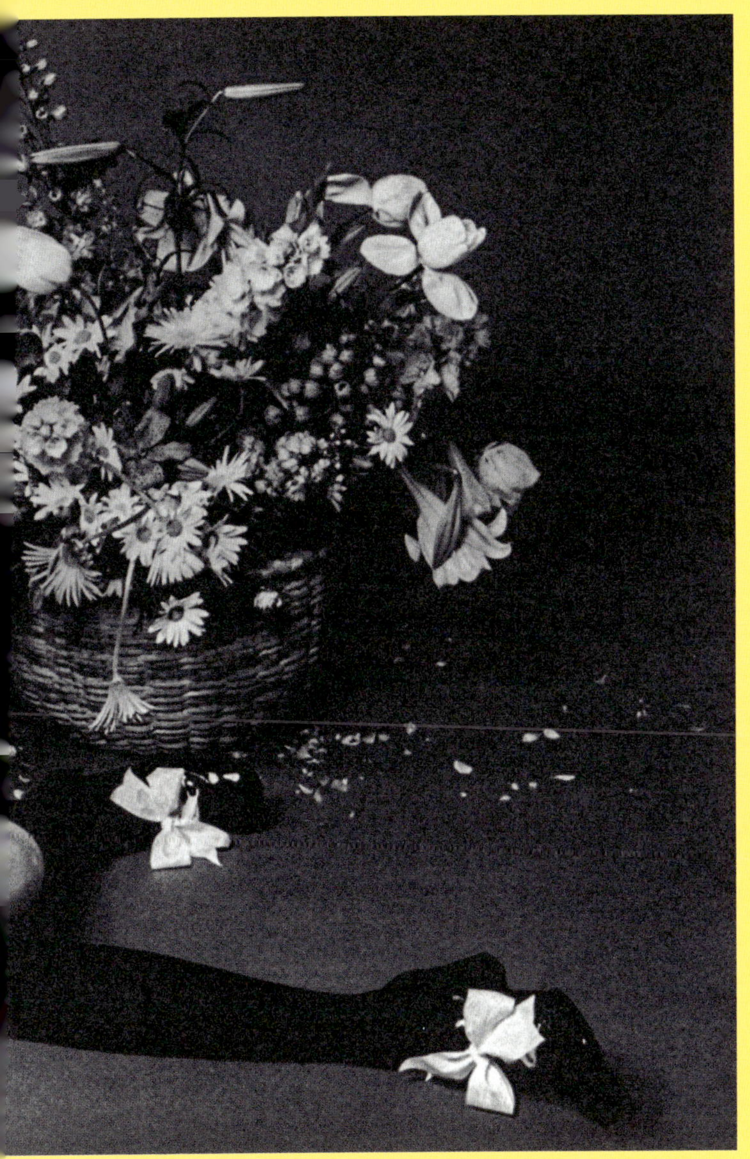

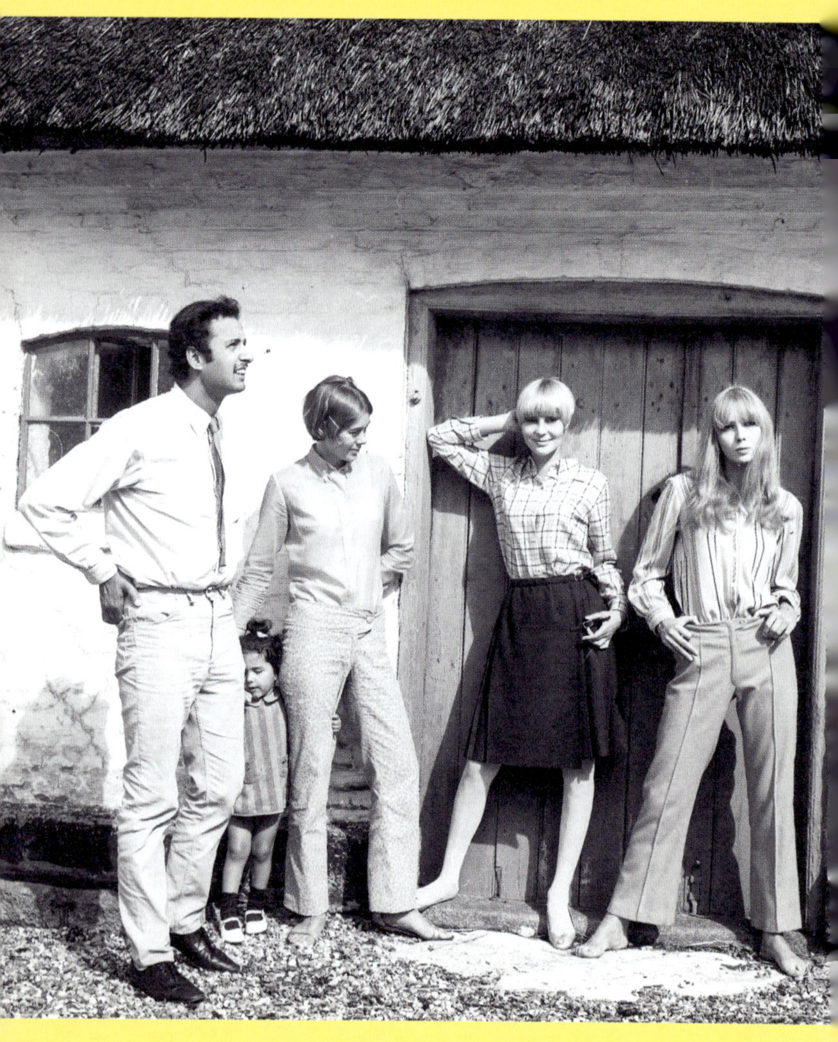

Above: Søs and Ib Drasbæk admire two models posing in the couple's designs, 1966.

Opposite: Fashion designer Bent Visti admires a sketch on the waterfront, 1964.

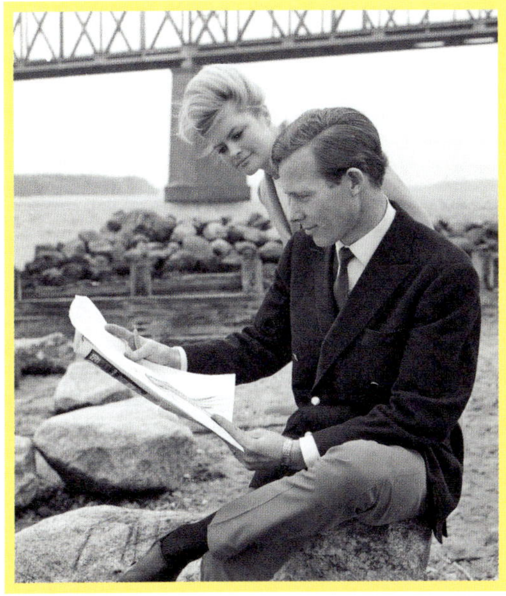

Then there was Dranella. The label was launched in 1956 by another husband-and-wife couple, Søs and Ib Drasbæk. Søs designed the clothes and Ib is said to have managed the manufacturing processes. The design duo pushed boundaries and used brighter colours and bold prints that many associated with the look of Londoners at the time that had not yet become popular in Denmark. Bent Visti is another key name in the group of apparel designers who are credited with shaking up the wardrobe of Copenhagen residents during this era. Visti is reported to have made a name for himself designing for Danish label Rivoli before heading to Paris to work for Dior. Together, this group helped to promote Danish design as something worthy of international attention and respect, and they continue to be a source of inspiration for modern Danish fashion houses with an affinity for all things bright and bold.

chapter 3

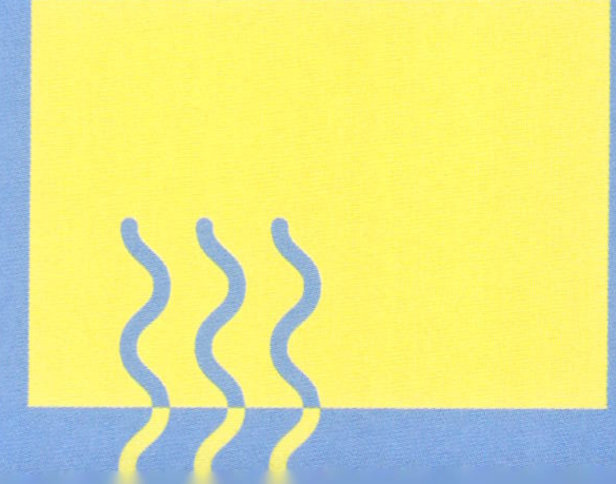

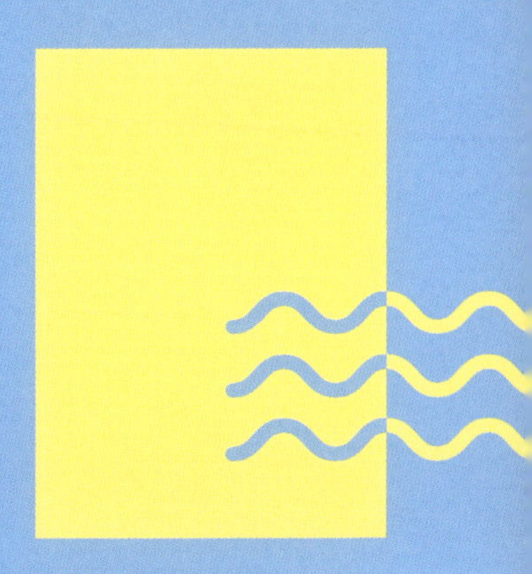

MOVING INTO A NEW MILLENNIUM

By the latter part of the twentieth century, the reputation of Denmark was growing internationally as a key player in two new areas – music and models. Brigitte Nielsen was one of the first Danish models to become a household name after spending much of the 1980s modelling for some of the era's top magazines and photographers. This was before going on to act in films alongside some of the top stars of the time, including Sylvester Stallone – who she would go on to marry and divorce.

In 1994, Sannie Carlson (better known by her music moniker Whigfield) went straight to number one in the charts with the single 'Saturday Night'. Before her success in music, Carlson studied fashion design in Copenhagen. In 1997, Danish pop group Aqua took the charts by storm with their single 'Barbie Girl'. This tendency for Copenhagen and wider Danish culture to attract global attention would continue through to the early 2000s.

"The development of the Danish fashion scene – primarily the design-led scene in the Copenhagen area – did not happen in isolation."
Katrina Sark

Alongside Helena Christensen, Brigitte Nielsen is often regarded as one of the first Danish models to become a household name, seen here in 1987.

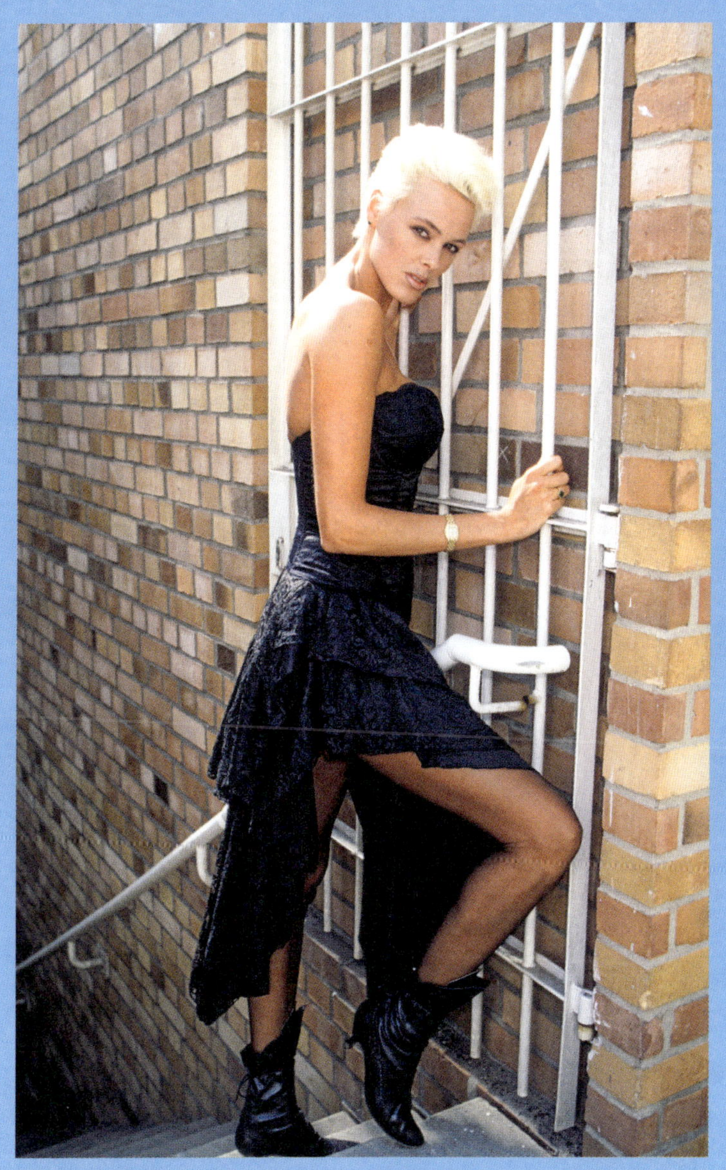

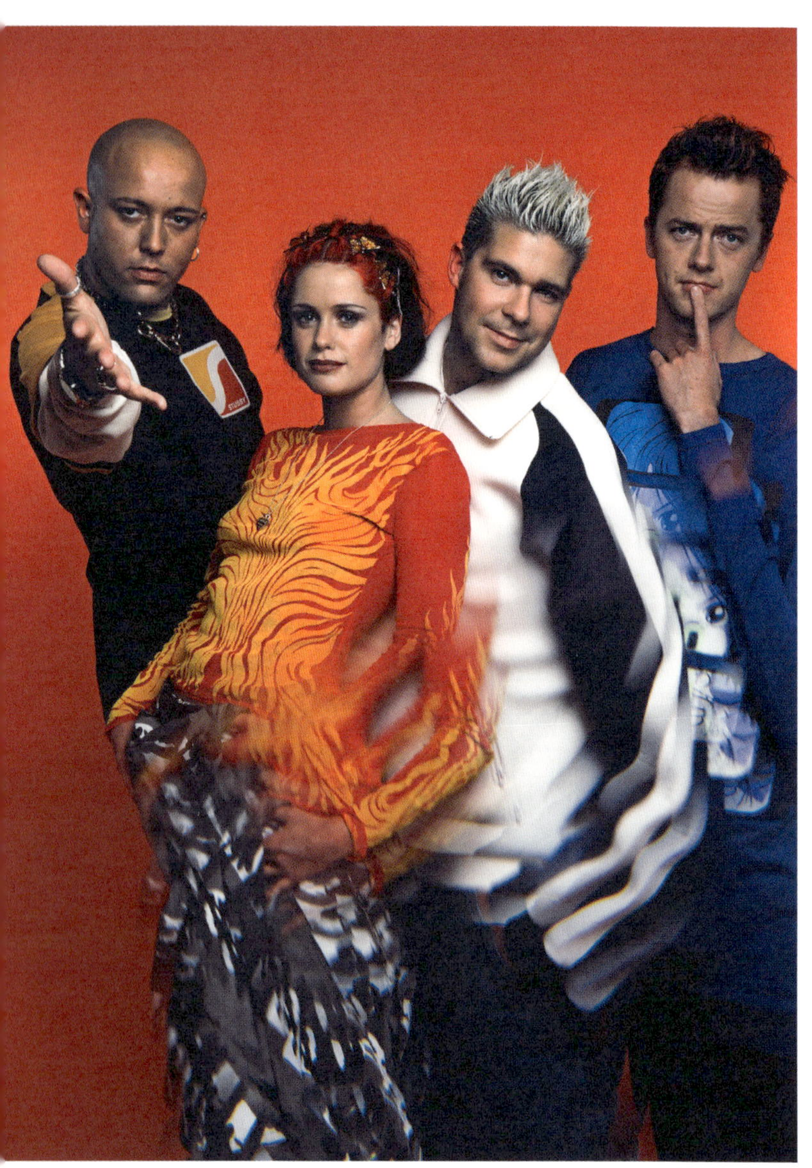

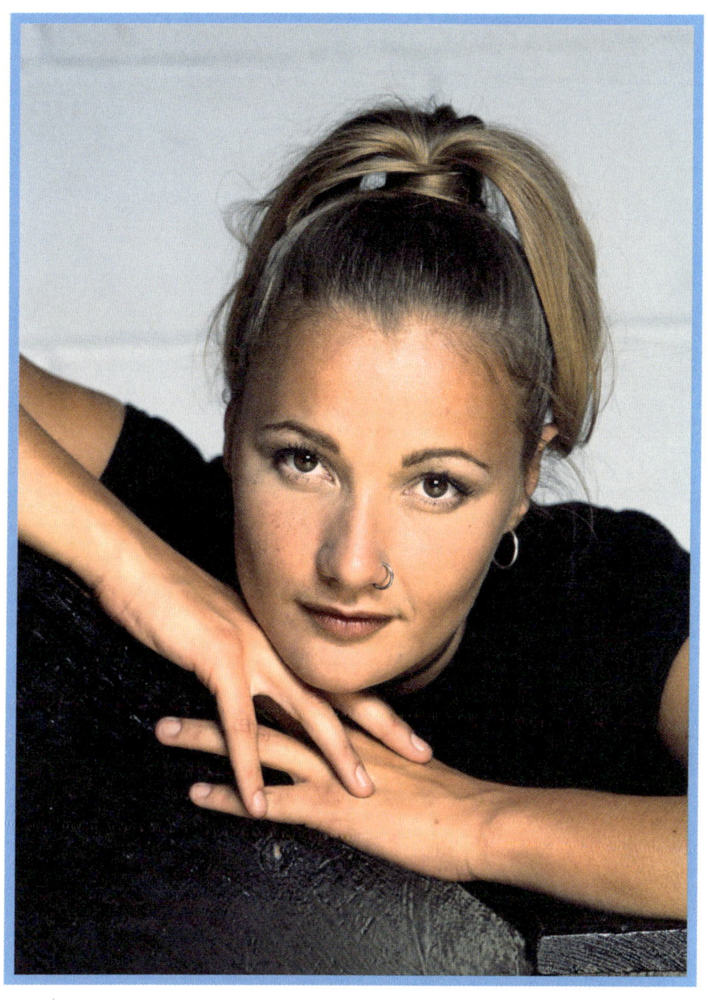

Opposite: Pop group Aqua is one of Denmark's most notable musical exports, formed in Copenhagen in 1995.

Above: Sannie Carlson (better known as Whigfield) helped put Danish pop on the map with her 1994 hit 'Saturday Night'.

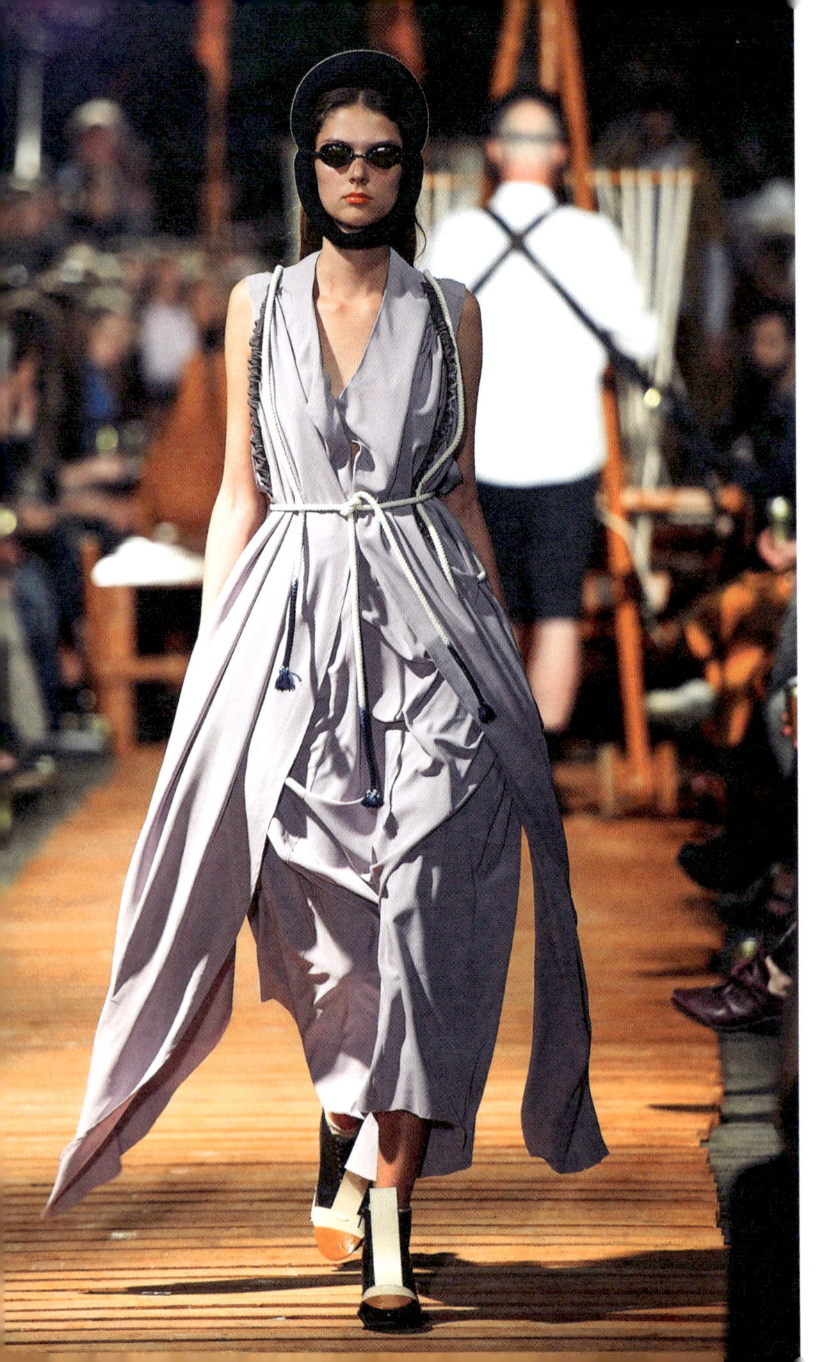

As Denmark's reputation was growing as a creative powerhouse internationally, Copenhagen was fast becoming a thriving spot for cosmopolitan affairs from fine dining to refined design. Katrina Sark discusses this pivotal period in her book on Copenhagen, stating: "The development of the Danish fashion scene – primarily the design-led scene in the Copenhagen area – did not happen in isolation." Sark refers to the films of Lars von Trier and Thomas Vinterberg, and the New Nordic Cuisine movement that saw restaurant NOMA draw further attention towards what was going on in Copenhagen. Sark goes on to say: "In this respect, branding and researching Danish fashion as something particular and locally flavoured was in tune with its time and the general societal, economic and cultural currents of the period."

With Denmark getting comfortable in the limelight, creativity in Copenhagen was at an all-time high, likely serving as a key motive for aspiring fashion designers across the capital. Brands like Ganni, Wood Wood, By Malene Birger, Henrik Vibskov and Samsøe Samsøe were all formed in the early 2000s, proving that creative talent in Copenhagen was reaching new levels.

A model walks the runway at the Henrik Vibskov show at Copenhagen Fashion Week in August 2010.

CREATIVE COPENHAGEN

In 2004, a travelling exhibition curated by the Danish Design Center titled *UNIK: Danish Fashion* garnered more attention for designers from the Scandinavian country. Fashion writer Lotte Freddie stated in the exhibition's catalogue: "Danish fashion design is moving very well at the moment! We stand with a generation of new designers who, with inspiration from a modern, globalized and individualized world, are bursting with self-confidence and show results that make professionals around the globe open their eyes."

The early 2000s also marked a time when skate culture was gaining traction across much of the Western world. But unlike many other major cities that saw skateboarding as something of a nuisance that posed a threat to the status quo, Copenhagen embraced this branch of youth culture by quickly incorporating skate-friendly spaces into the city's infrastructure. The local skateparks became go-to spots for skateboarders and onlookers alike, much like football pitches were appreciated in other cities. Another area that enriched the city's creative scene during this period was the graffiti scene. The Danish capital boasted a wide selection of spaces that functioned as "semi-legal" for street artists looking to demonstrate their craft. Spots like the Sydhavnen Hall of Fame became iconic for showcasing some of the city's best graffiti artists' works and continued to be a popular spot until its demolition in 2013.

Those from the skate and graffiti scenes have played key roles in shaping some of Denmark's most-loved clothing

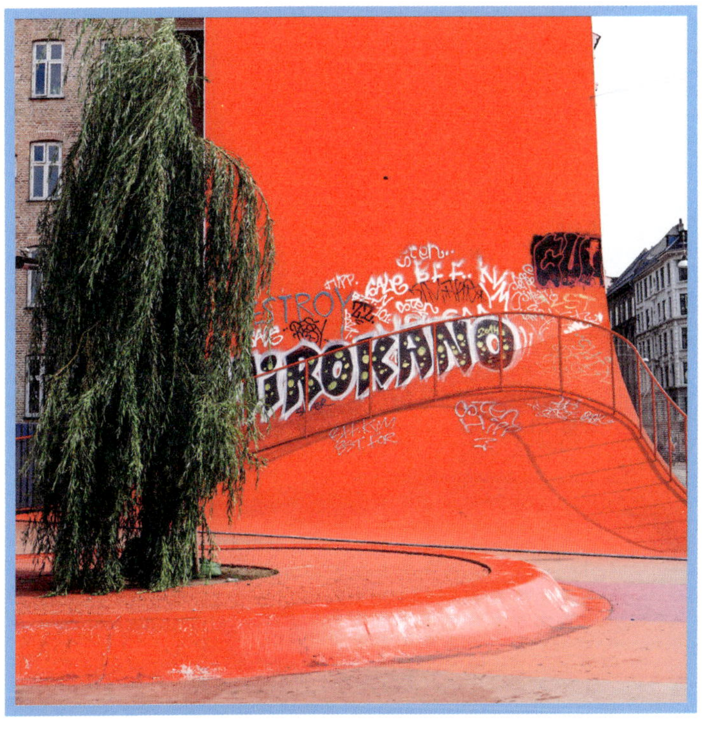

Superkilen Park's "red square" in Nørrebro, a skateboarding spot in Copenhagen.

labels, with pro skater Silas Adler co-founding Soulland, and Ulrik Pedersen, founder of NN.07 and Sunflower, being active in the graffiti scene in the 1990s and 2000s. Sigurd Bank, founder of mfpen, was also a keen skater and graffiti fan around this time. The list goes on. These branches of youth culture are still influential in other aspects of Danish fashion too, with brands like Han Kjøbenhavn using graffiti'd walls as the backdrop to their runway shows, or Baum und Pferdgarten using graffiti print across their SS24 collection.

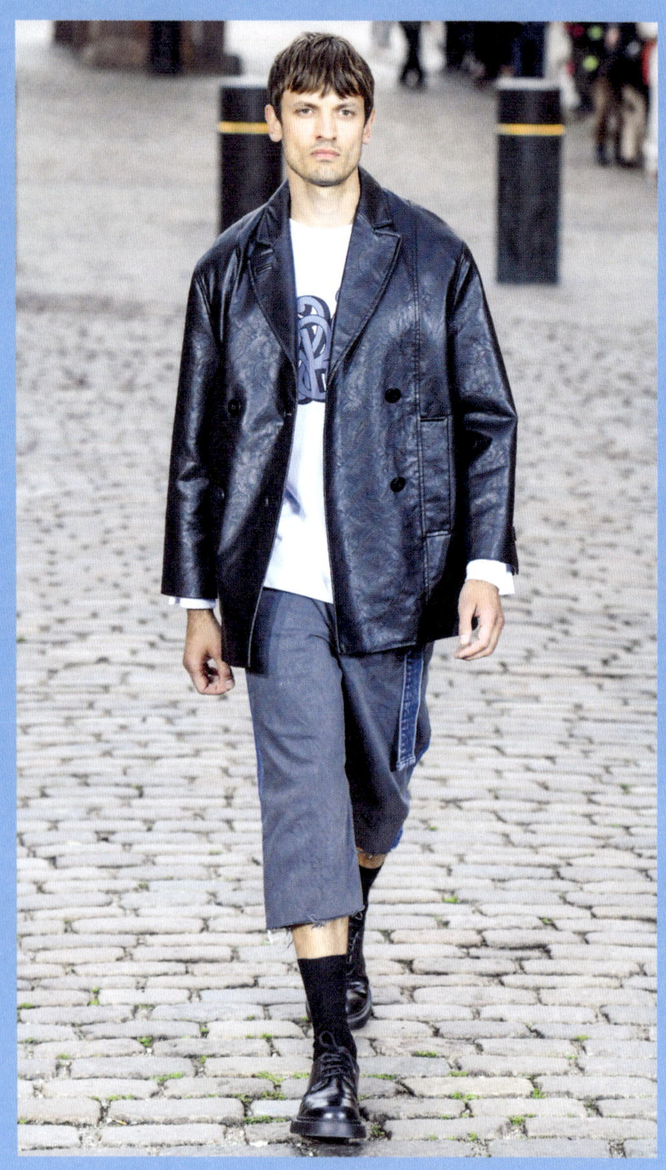

"At that time, the skateboard scene was much more linked to the worlds of graffiti, music and Christiania"
Silas Adler

Due to its modest size and geographical location, Copenhagen was the perfect setting for incubating a thriving youth culture; tucked away from the melting pot of other European capitals enough to build its own distinct identity while still connected enough to incorporate the outside influences that supported growth and creativity in the city. While other fashion capitals had deep-rotted traditions to either carry on or revolt against, Copenhagen's fashion scene in the 2000s didn't face this issue. From an international vantage point, Danish fashion had the privilege of using this period to make a name for itself by fusing the famous Danish charm with the creative energy that had reached new heights in the 1990s and 2000s, and showcase that in the form of apparel for the world to fall in love with.

The city of Copenhagen supported this brewing movement through the launch of incentives like "Meat and Creativity" in 2005, which encouraged collaboration between gastronomy, artists and designers of various disciplines to come together in the city's Meatpacking District (known as Kødbyen). By 2008, this exciting energy was recognized by culture aficionados across the globe, including *New York Times* journalist Stephen Whitlock, who said in an article about Copenhagen: "The city has evolved into an exciting scramble of ideas about everything from furniture to food."

Baum und Pferdgarten's Spring/Summer 2024 collection, "A Postcard from Copenhagen", took inspiration from the city's graffiti scene for its print offering.

"Being creative in Copenhagen means having a hand in art, design, music and cuisine, all at the same time."
Stephen Whitlock

Beyond the formation of some of the leading Copenhagen-based labels, the fashion scene of the Danish capital would also be defined by a few key movements during this period. One of the first to occur would be in 2005, when the Danish Design Society announced that the Danish Fashion Institute was to launch.

By 2006, textiles and clothing was ranked as Denmark's fourth largest export, a testament to the sector's substantial growth and burgeoning international interest. It was that same year when another key shift would take place: the very first Copenhagen Fashion Week (CPHFW). Though we know from the previous chapter that its history dates back to the 1960s, 2006 marked the transition to the fashion week we know today. It was in the same year that CPH Vision would launch, a more trend-focused branch of the Copenhagen International Fashion Fair (CIFF). These two entities would play essential roles in attracting fashion-forward audiences to Copenhagen and help establish the city as a primary destination for those in the know when it comes to all things fashion.

Danish fashion journalist Lotte Freddie looked back on this inaugural event in 2006. In an interview with the Danish publication *Eurowoman,* she recalls the launch of Copenhagen Fashion Week at the famous Town Hall: "That Rådhushallen was chosen for this was clear proof of how far the Danish fashion industry had come – not only in the world, but also in Danish society."

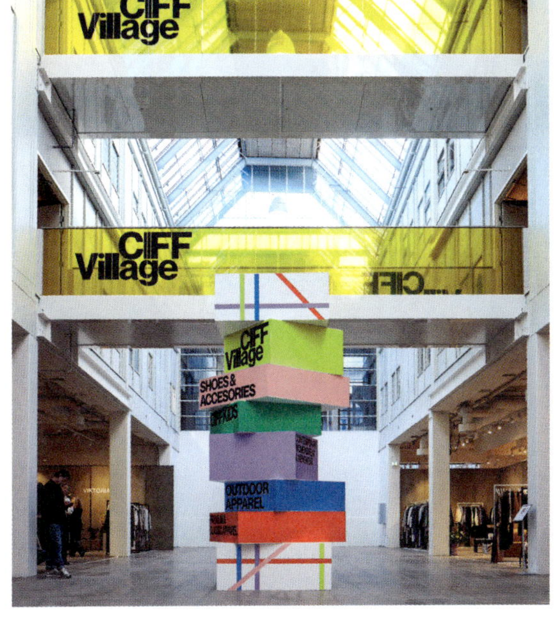

Copenhagen International Fashion Fair (CIFF) plays a key role in showcasing some of the most inspiring Danish fashion labels on the market. The offering is laid out across the 20,000 square-metre CIFF Village, pictured here in 2024.

Stylistically, the brands of this period were heavily leaning into the aesthetic that names like Mads Nørgaard Copenhagen were popularizing – understated, minimal and rife with clean lines. The Scandi boom meant brands like Wood Wood, Samsøe Samsøe and Won Hundred were bringing in global audiences. But by the mid-2010s, there would be a new influx of labels moving in to shake things up and bring them back to the colourful and eclectic roots of Denmark's mid-century boho designers. Sanne Sehested, founder of Danish womenswear label Gestuz, weighs in on this in a 2020 interview: "We used to be known for a very clean, minimalistic expression [...] but I think we have gotten braver when it comes to colours and patterns."

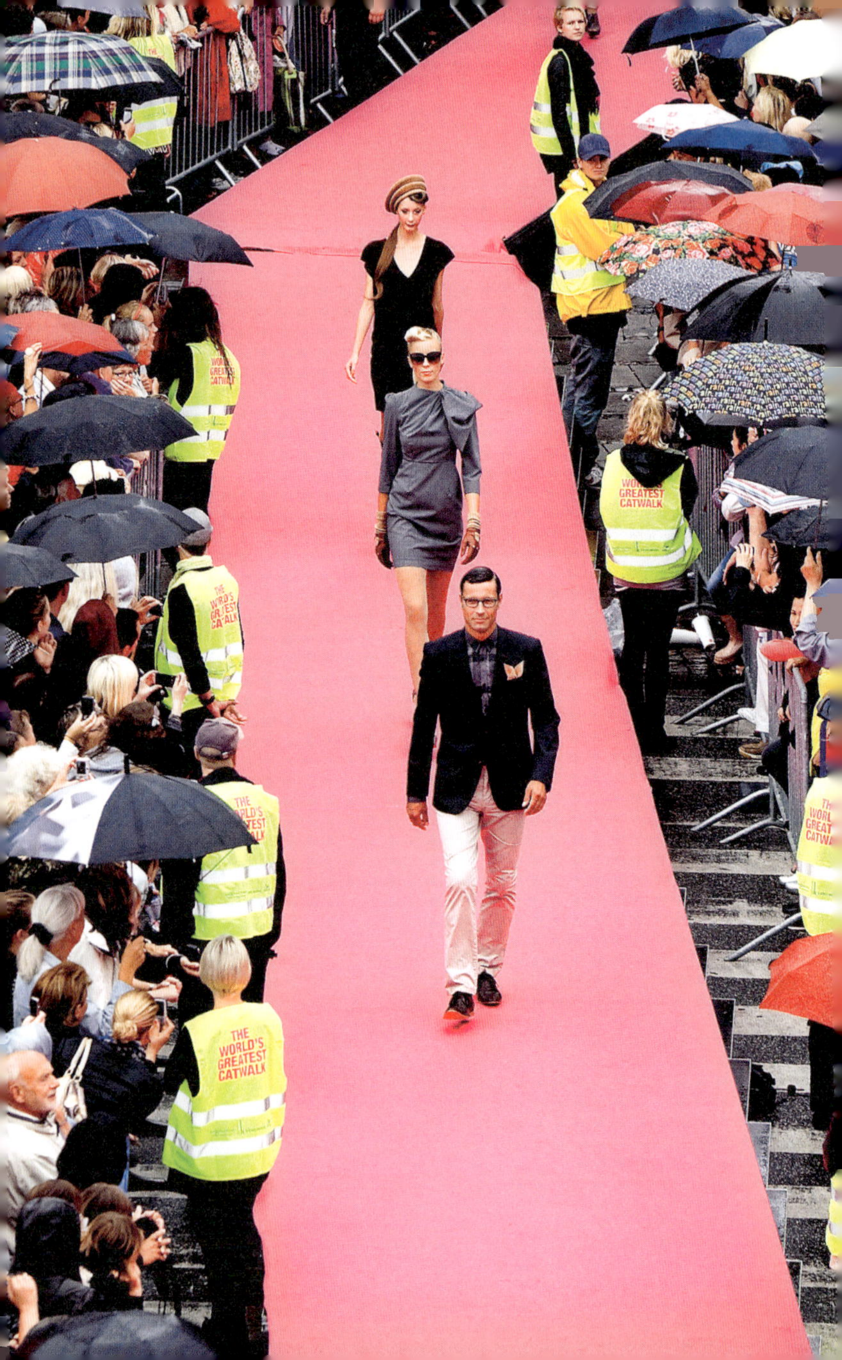
THE
WORLD'S
GREATEST
CATWALK
WORLD'S
GREATEST
CATWALK

A NEW FRONTIER FOR DANISH FASHION

"There is a relaxed and effortless approach to fashion that I believe makes Danish style relatable and desirable to everyone – It's the mix of old and new, comfort and couture"
Cecilie Bahnsen

By 2010, Copenhagen was capturing even more international attention. But what better way to increase this further than to host the world's longest catwalk? On 14 August, Copenhagen's famous Strøget street was transformed with a bright pink carpet at a total length of 1.6 kilometres.

Bold banners were hung in the area with the words "The World's Greatest Catwalk" plastered across them. The event attracted an estimated 100,000 onlookers who witnessed the happening in person (while being streamed by CNN to viewers in New York's Times Square) and featured designs from some of Denmark's most exciting labels. Supermodel Helena Christensen co-hosted the event and shared her love for the Danish fashion industry, admiring it for being

Models walk the world's longest catwalk as part of the closing event of the 2010 edition of Copenhagen Fashion Week.

"functional and unique, democratic fashion, built on values in many ways characterizing the Danes". This event would attract worldwide attention to the Danish fashion scene from both fashion insiders and the general public alike, helping cement Danish fashion brands as vital players across the international market.

Nearly 15 years later, Copenhagen Fashion Week continues to be held across the city twice a year, highlighting not just the best of Scandinavian fashion but also platforming innovative collaborations and showcasing the Danish capital's community spirit. Aside from its impressive dedication to sustainability (which we'll delve into in chapter 5), Copenhagen Fashion Week has become a favourite for fashion lovers around the globe due to its refreshing take on what an event like this can be. The fusion of established heritage labels with young talent creates an environment that values creativity over status and pushes to rewrite the rules regarding how the fashion world should operate. For those two weeks of the year, CPHFW transforms the city into a haven of immersive catwalk shows and collaborative events that reflect the Danish mentality of rejecting elitism and embracing collaborative energy. As fashion editor Oyindamola Animashaun remarks: "A beacon of accessibility and inclusivity, providing fashion enthusiasts from all corners of the globe with an entry point into the world of high fashion."

Danish stylist Mie Juel Engel and writer Marie Hindkær enjoy a break between shows at Copenhagen Fashion Week, 2020.

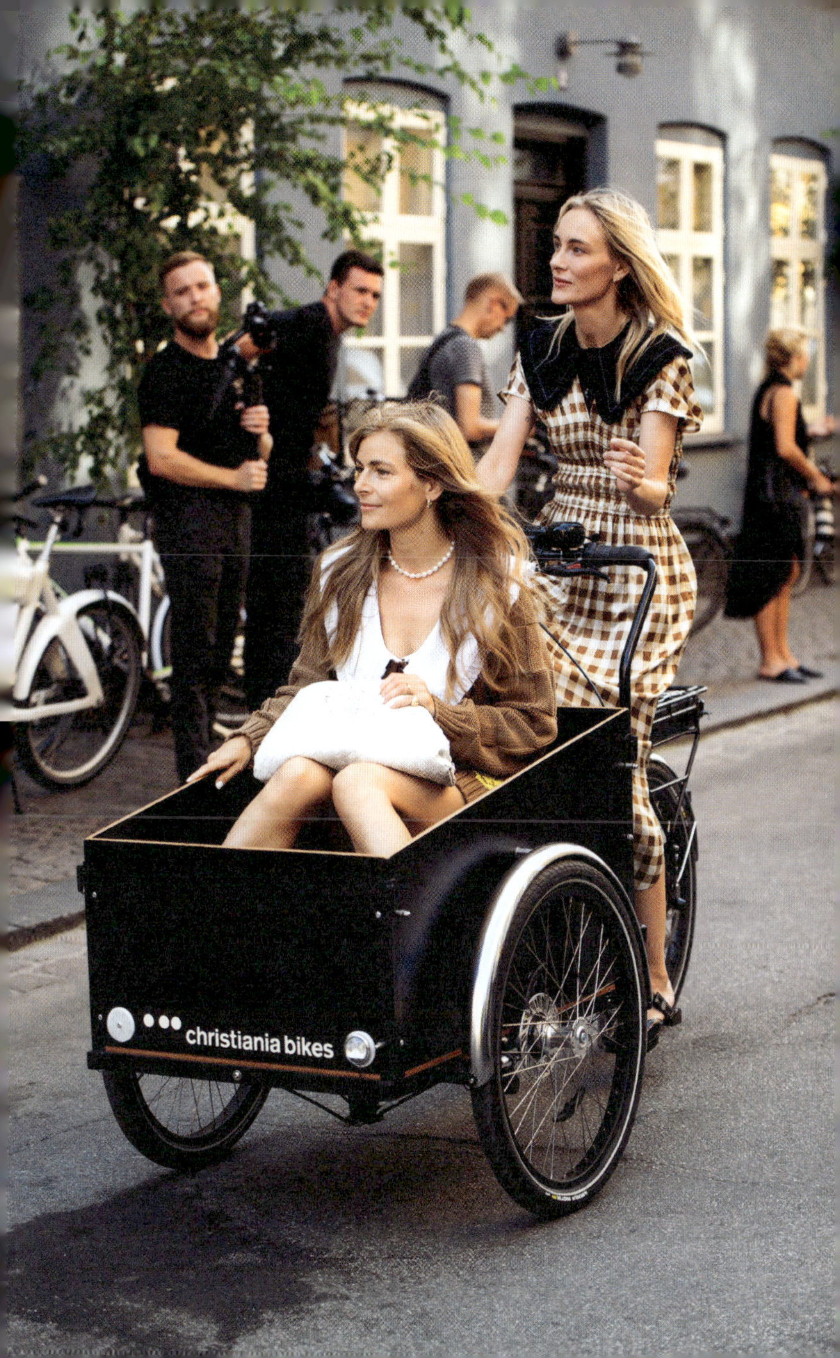
christiania bikes

chapter 4

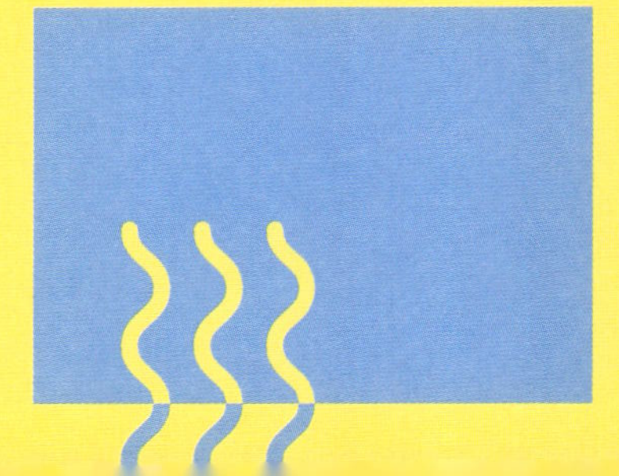

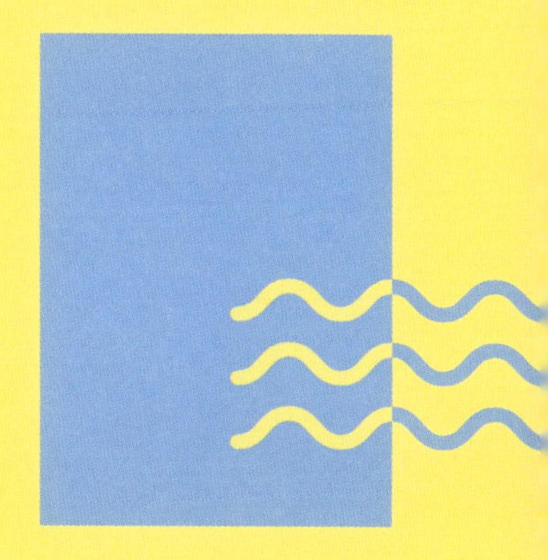

THE KEY NAMES

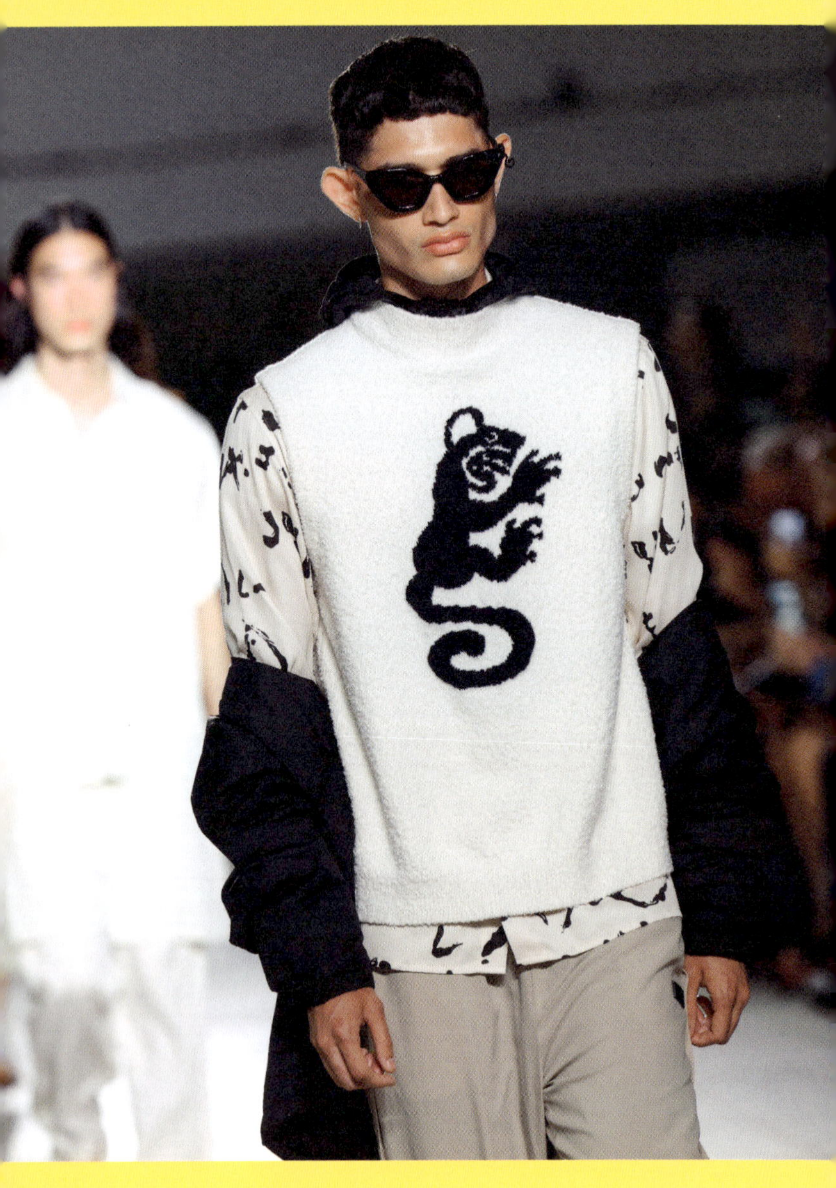

Once known for being a monochrome haven, the Danish fashion industry has evolved into a place that offers semiotic richness through a vast array of hues, textures, cuts and references. While there's still a firm place for heritage labels and classic styles, Copenhagen has embraced a wide range of approaches to fashion and style, incorporating everything from bold and bright whimsical looks to clean-cut tailoring and sportswear-inspired staples.

Aside from their geographical roots, many of these Copenhagen brands tend to also share a dedication to accessibility that is less commonplace among the fashion houses in Milan or Paris. The Danish sensibility of being a socialist nation with some of the most admired welfare policies in the world can be felt while browsing the rails of even the country's most aspirational designer shops. In this chapter, we'll explore some of the top names that have helped form Danish style in all its glory and played key roles in gaining worldwide respect by fusing aspiration and accessibility, resulting in the formation of one of the most style-centric cities in the world.

Models walk the runway for Danish label Soulland at Pitti Immagine Uomo 102 in Florence, Italy, in June 2022.

CULT COOLNESS

Hailed by *METAL Magazine* as "the city's most distinct alternative fashion voice", in 2008 Jannik Wikkelsø Davidsen founded Han Kjøbenhavn, which started as a sunglasses label. The brand has since grown into one of Denmark's most favoured exports when it comes to avant-garde style.

Since venturing into the world of apparel, the Copenhagen-based label has become a favourite among A-listers (Julia Fox and Cardi B are notable fans) while continuing to push boundaries and shift the public perception of Scandinavian fashion with its dark, structural styles, unexpected casting and immersive runway shows. Though Wikkelsø has been known to note international influences for his collections, the impact of the Danish capital is evident both in the location of the brand's HQ and the name itself – *Han* meaning "he", the Danish pronoun for men, and Kjøbenhavn being a play on the Danish word for Copenhagen (København), with the j being added for stylistic reasons.

At just 19 years old, life-long friends Barbara Potts and Cathrine Saks set out with a simple enough mission: to create their perfect coat that went beyond what they refer to as "the total monochrome status quo". Under the title Saks Potts, the duo has produced some of the most instantly recognizable styles in the Danish fashion scene

Han Kjøbenhavn proves their affinity for dark design on the runway at Copenhagen Fashion in February 2024.

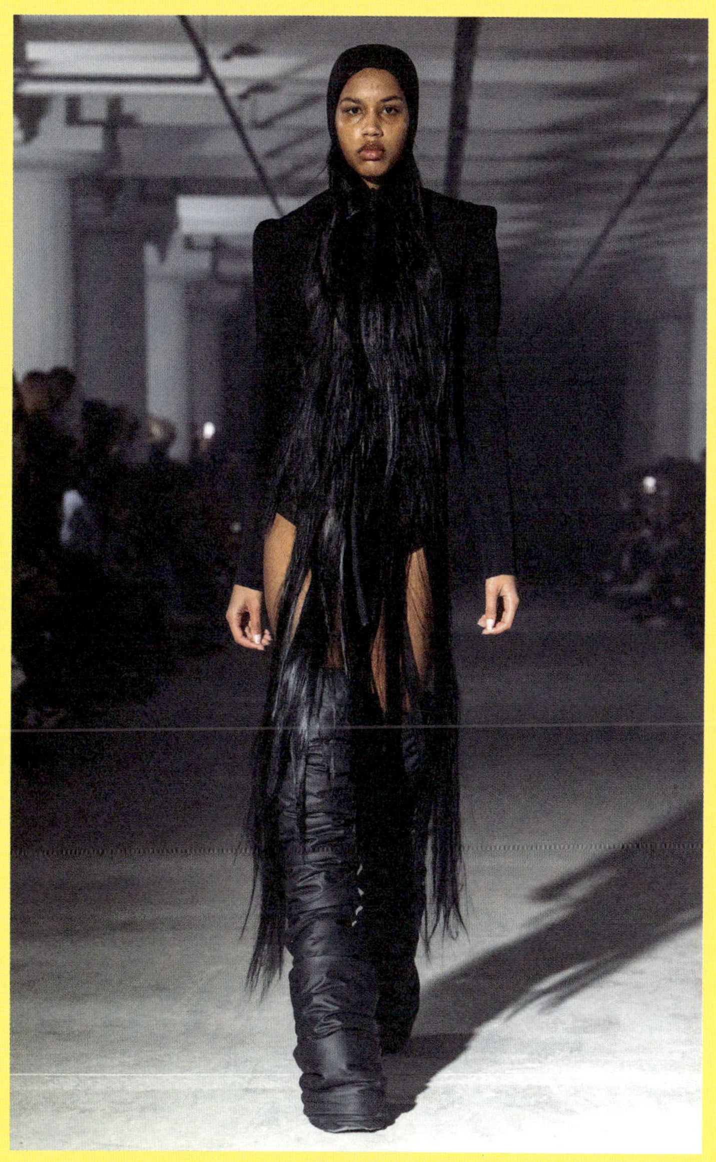

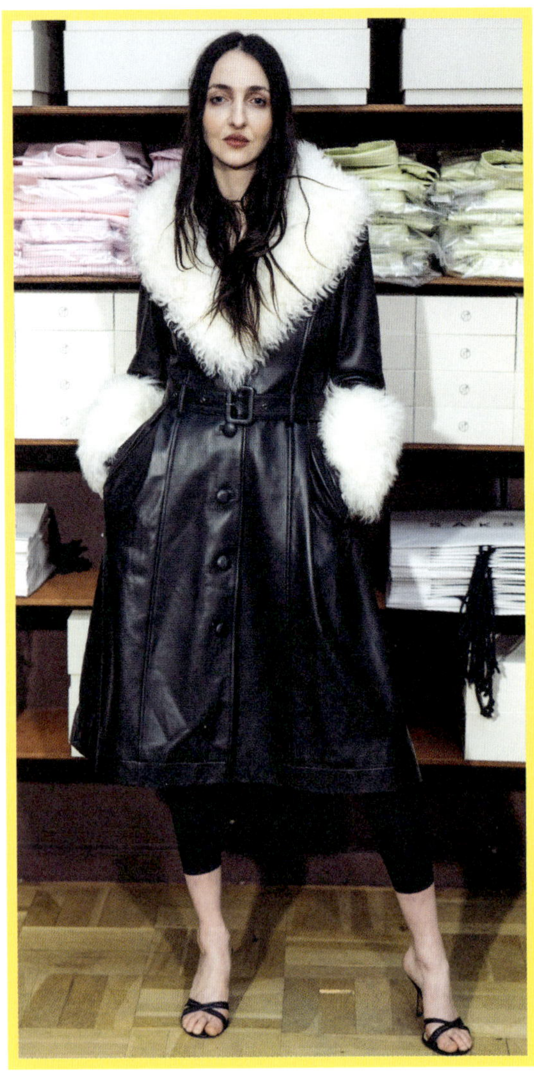

Model shows off one of Saks Potts' coveted coat styles as a part of the label's presentation at Copenhagen Fashion Week in January 2024.

and beyond. Their leather jackets with fluffy fur trims have become a favourite for It girls across the globe, inspiring plenty of copycat looks (because you know what they say). The label's fluorescent glitter two-pieces have also gained viral status in recent years, furthering the pair's agenda of offering eye-catching looks that steer clear of the modesty previously associated with the Scandinavian fashion market. But functionality is also a key focus, as Barbara Potts notes in a 2024 interview with *PUSS PUSS Magazine*: "When you're from Copenhagen, it's all about bicycling and practical details; it needs to be functional. Many of our jackets always have numerous pockets for added convenience." Since debuting at Copenhagen Fashion Week in 2016, Saks Potts has used its shows to pay homage to its Danish roots. Most notably, the designers staged a show outside Arne Jacobsen's home for the Fall/Winter 2021 collection and Copenhagen's Kongens Nytorv for the Spring/Summer 2023 collection.

Soulland's co-founder Silas Adler is now one of Denmark's most respected creative names. But in 2002, Adler was a 17-year-old high-school dropout, spending his days working at a restaurant, skateboarding and making T-shirts during his time off. Jacob Kampp Berliner joined Soulland in 2006 and took the label to new heights, solidifying spots at fashion weeks across the world and playing a key role in cementing some of the collaborations that helped shape Soulland's reputation for being a purveyor of playful streetwear-inspired styles. From Hello Kitty to *Peanuts* and Kronenbourg 1664 (yes, the French beer), Soulland's catalogue of collaborators proves the label's dedication to bringing different worlds together in harmony; just as Adler helped bring together the skate world and the fashion world in the label's early days. "The community aspect of skateboarding is my main inspiration for everything in life," Adler told *Vogue* in a 2020 interview.

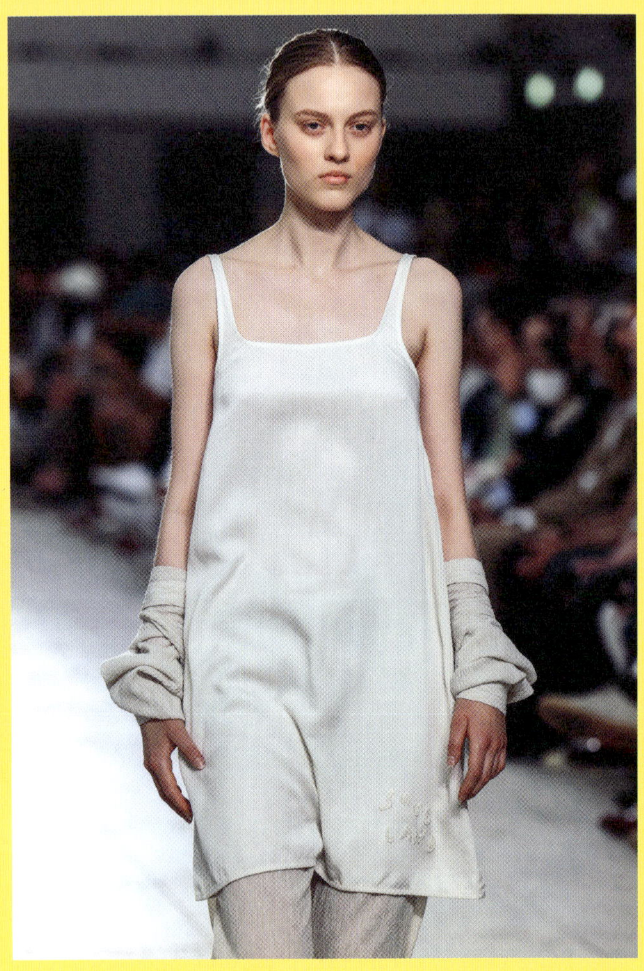

Above: Model walks the runway at Soulland's Spring/Summer 2023 show at Pitti Immagine Uomo 102 in Florence, Italy, in June 2022.

Opposite: The Spring/Summer 2023 season was the first where Soulland took a totally unisex approach. Pictured here is one the label's looks on the runway at Pitti Immagine Uomo 102 in Florence, Italy, in June 2022.

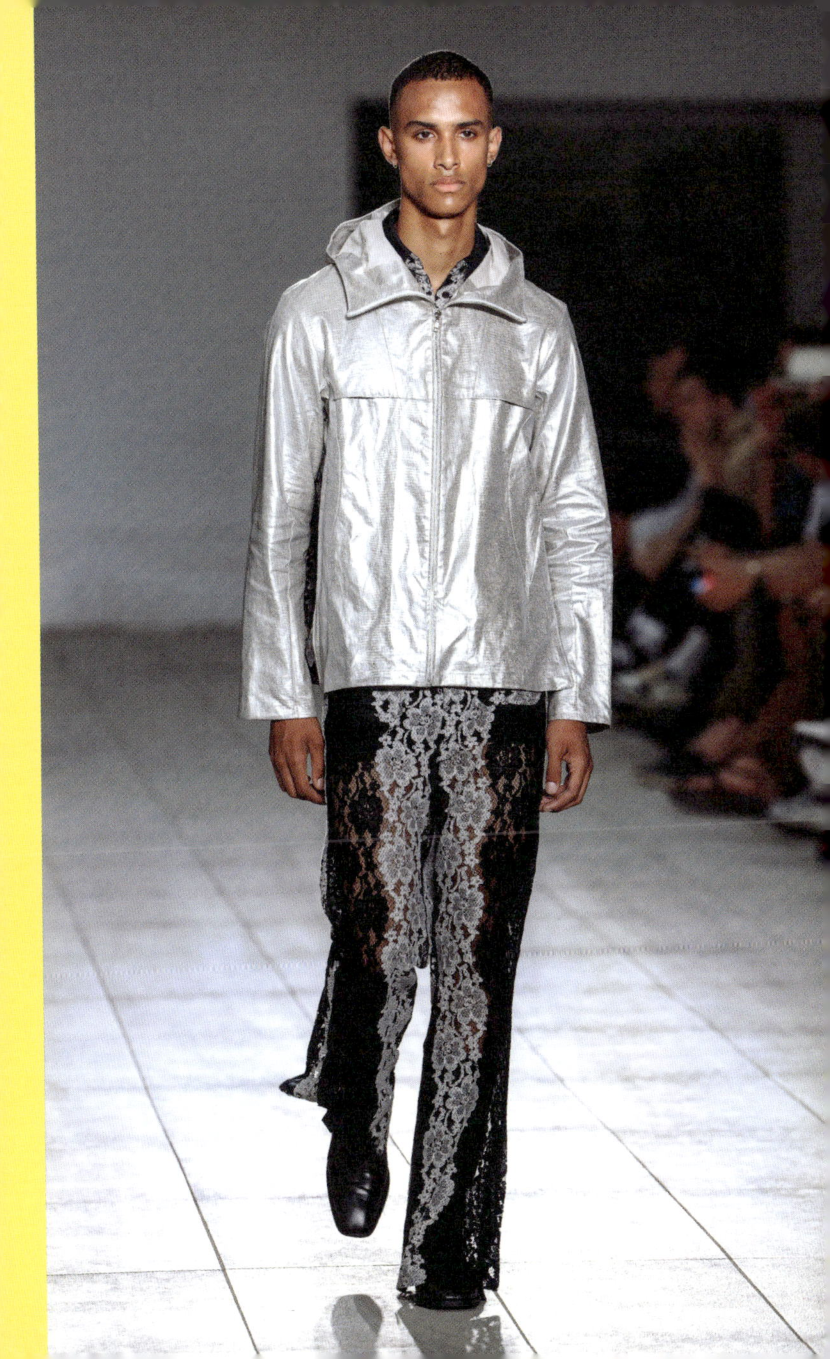

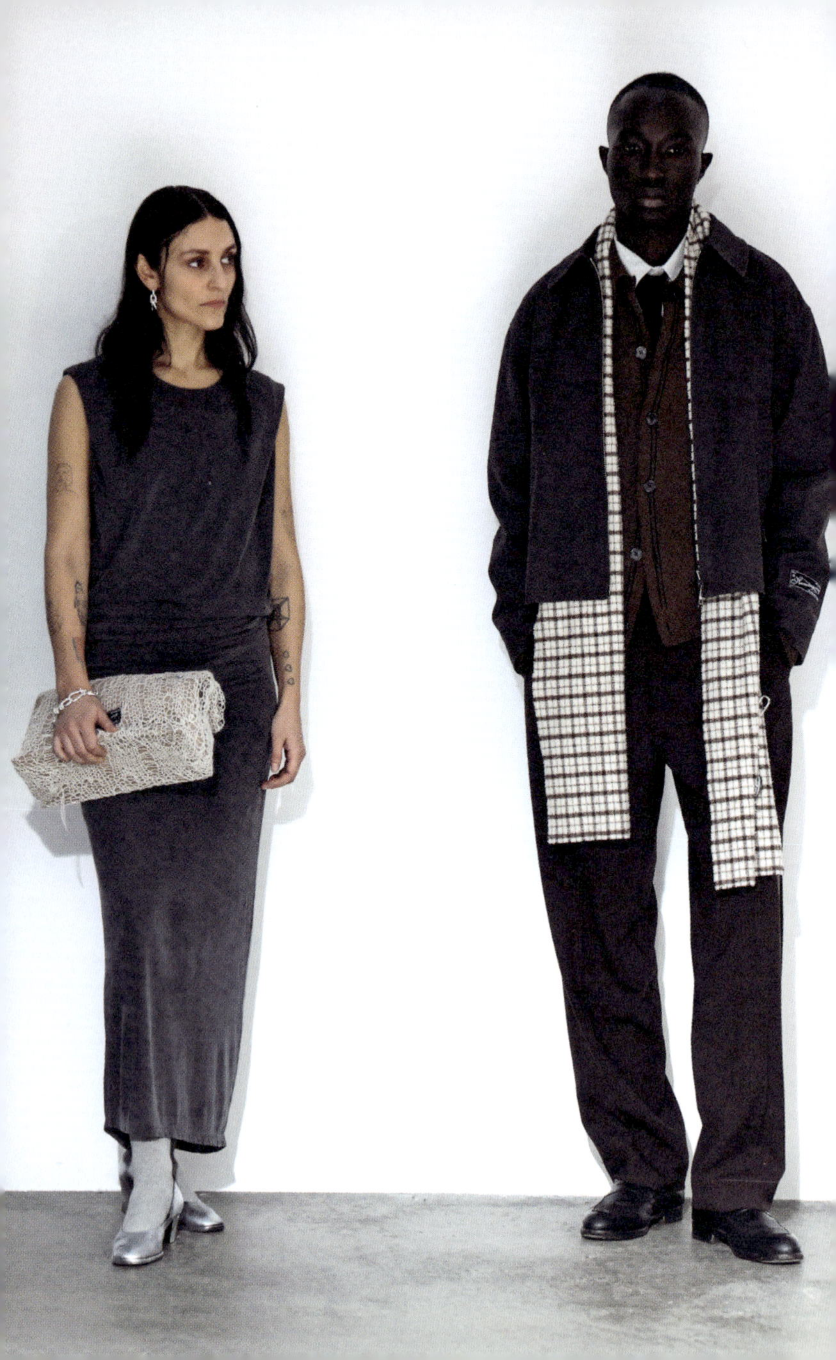

Another Danish name that proves the power that authenticity and simplicity can have within the apparel game is mfpen. Led by Sigurd Bank, the independent label was born out of Bank's desire to utilize deadstock fabrics to create pieces that reimagine traditional styles. "Personally, I hate people who wear suits because of what they stand for but I love the suit. It's the same suit, but we challenge those status symbols," Bank told *Hypebeast* writer Jack Stanley in a 2022 interview. Challenging those symbols is what Bank does best. References to hardcore music, graffiti and skateboarding are alive and well throughout the visuals that accompany mfpen's collections – it makes sense that its shop opening event during Copenhagen Fashion Week SS25 had one of the best playlists heard at a fashion event in a long time. The label fuses together innovative materials and unfussy silhouettes, brought to life with off-kilter styling for a distinct flavour of cool that has won the label plenty of fans since its 2015 inception – and the numbers are ever-growing.

Models show off mfpen's understated styles at Copenhagen Fashion Week in January 2024.

NOTABLE CLASSICS

The term "classic" in terms of Danish fashion could be seen as rather complicated. But for many, these brands can be seen as a good place to start. One of the first Danish labels to find itself in the wardrobes of international fashion lovers was Birger Christensen.

Starting out in 1869 as a humble alternations shop on Østergade in Copenhagen's city centre, the label has grown into nothing short of a Danish fashion powerhouse. The family-run brand has gone through plenty of adjustments over the years but continues to be a household name for both those keen on traditional styles and those with a love for fresh and modern wares via its ROTATE and REMAIN lines, which are often hailed as Copenhagen Fashion Week favourites.

Opposite: In August 2020, REMAIN Birger Christensen presented its Spring/Summer 2021 collection in the courtyard of the city's Thorvaldsen Museum.

Overleaf: ROTATE Birger Christensen designers Jeanette Madsen and Thora Valdimars grace the runway with models to close the Autumn/Winter 2021 show as a part of Copenhagen Fashion Week in January 2020.

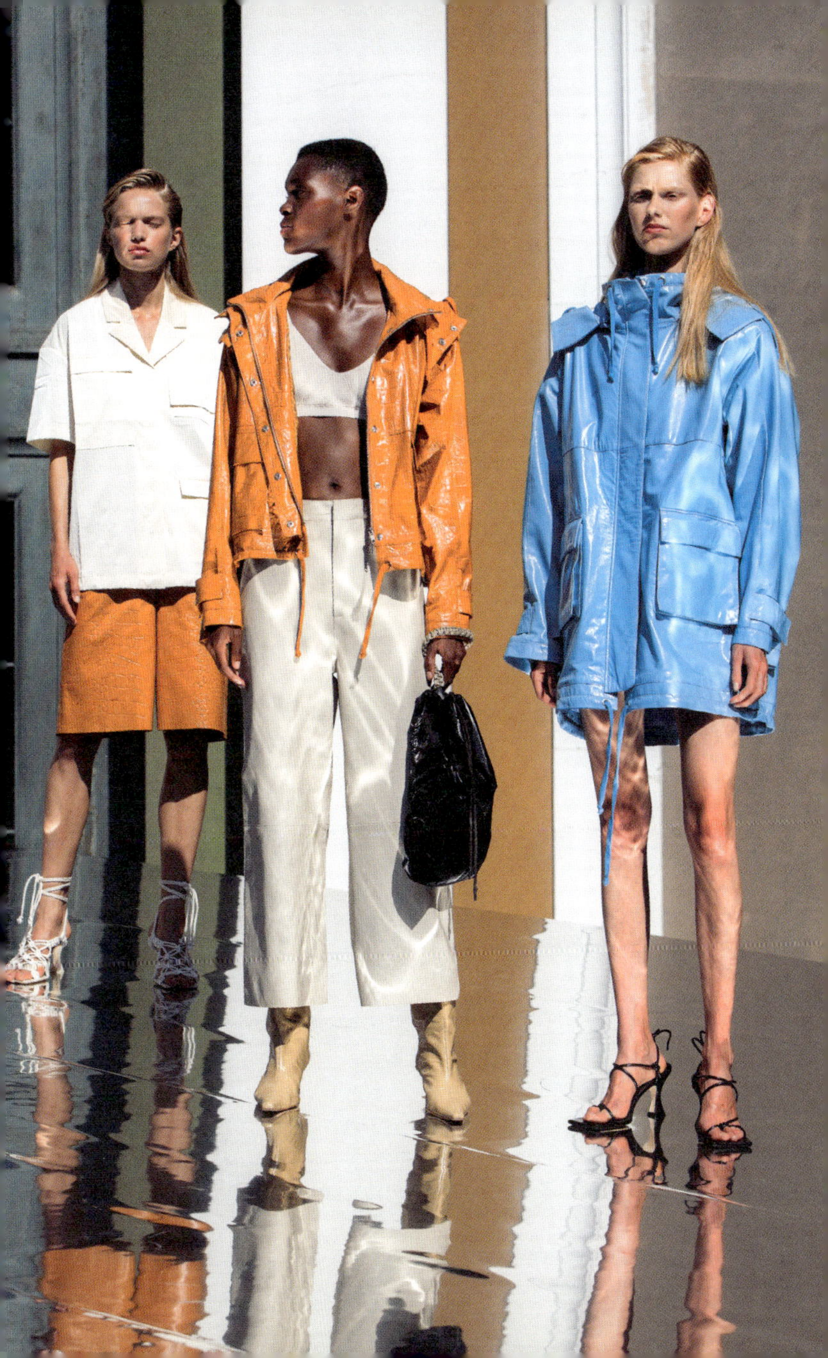

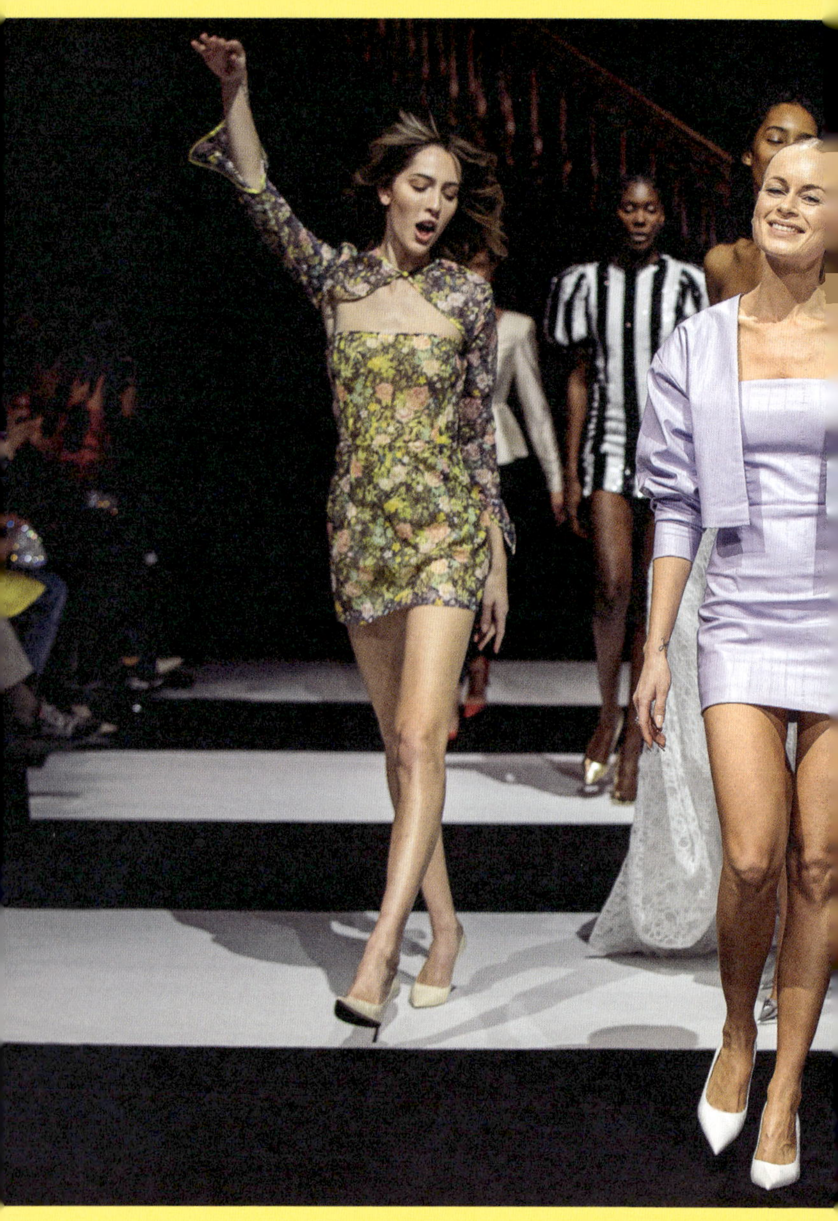

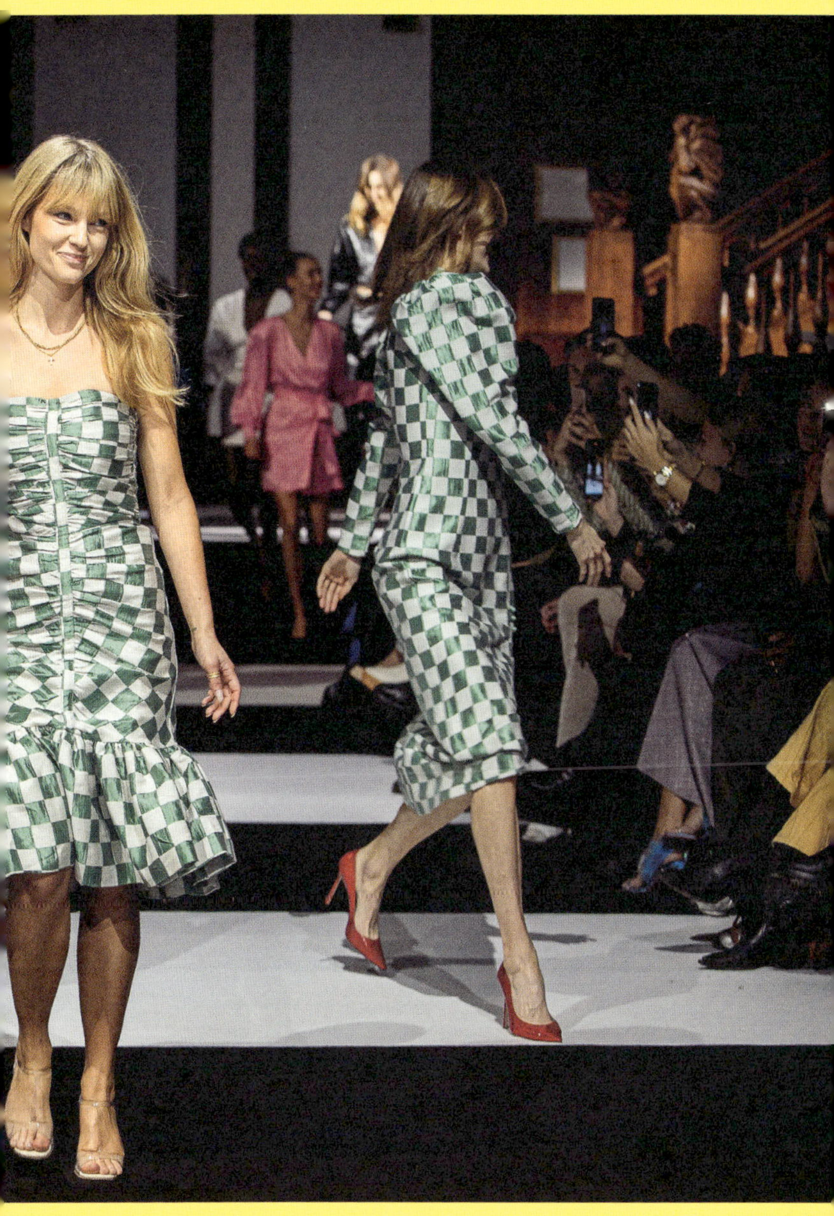

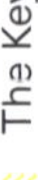

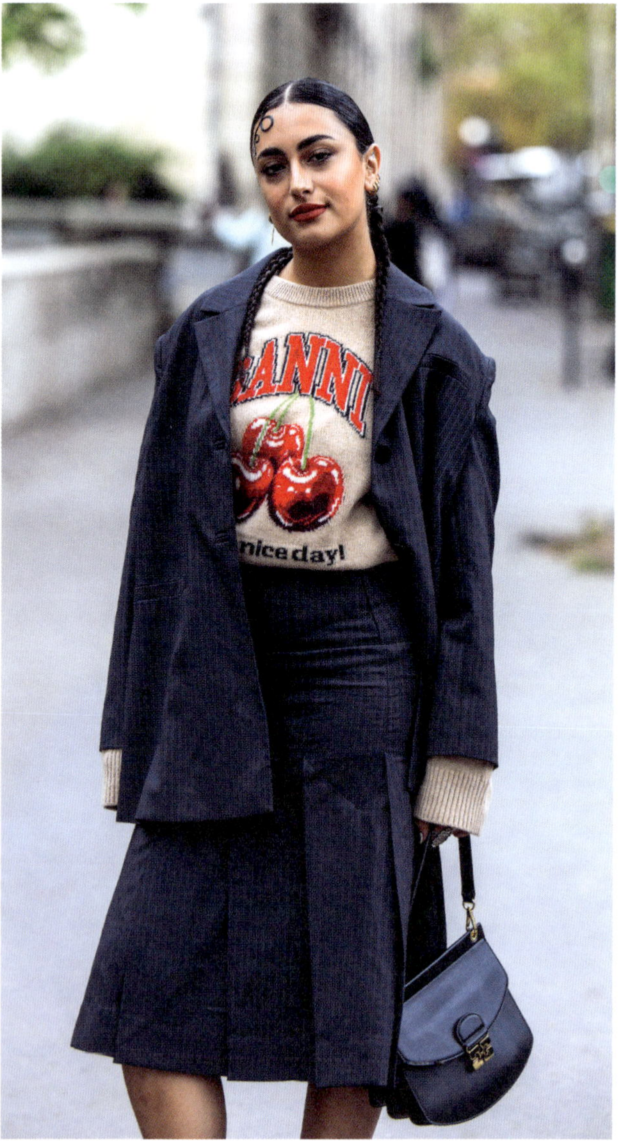

Having launched in 2000, Ganni has become an essential label not just for Danish fashion fans but fashion followers across the globe since its inception. Founder Frans Truelsen set out with the goal to create the perfect cashmere sweater. Though the label has delivered some impressive knitwear offerings over the years, it's gone far beyond that. In 2009, husband-and-wife duo Nicolaj and Ditte Reffstrup acquired the label and have since won the respect of apparel lovers internationally. The label is known for its playful yet wearable styles from graphic tees to patent faux-leather ballerina flats with bold buckle detailing that had the 2024 fashion week circuit in a chokehold. The Reffstrups credit their hometown with the label's success, explaining in a 2018 interview with *Porter*: "We're from Copenhagen; everything here seems very laid-back and cool – it's a very easy way of dressing. For example, we use our bikes every day, and you would never see a girl wearing a pair of heels on her bike, she would always be wearing a pair of sneakers and maybe have her heels in her basket."

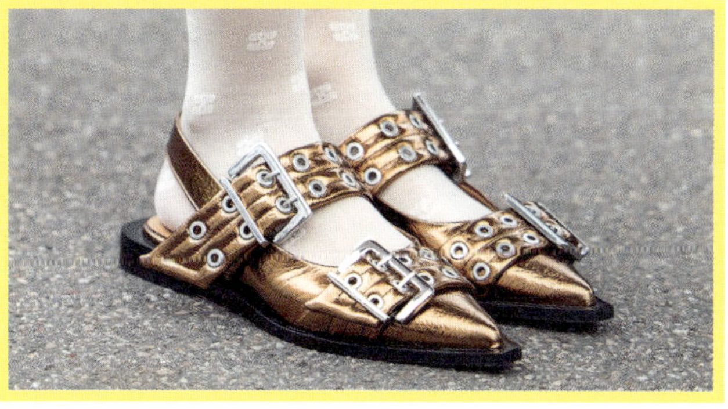

Opposite: A Paris Fashion Week guest proves Ganni's international reach, sporting a jumper from the label outside their show in September 2024.

Above: Ganni's "Buckle Ballerinas" have become a key piece in the Ganni catalogue, pictured here on the feet of a guest Paris Fashion Week in 2024.

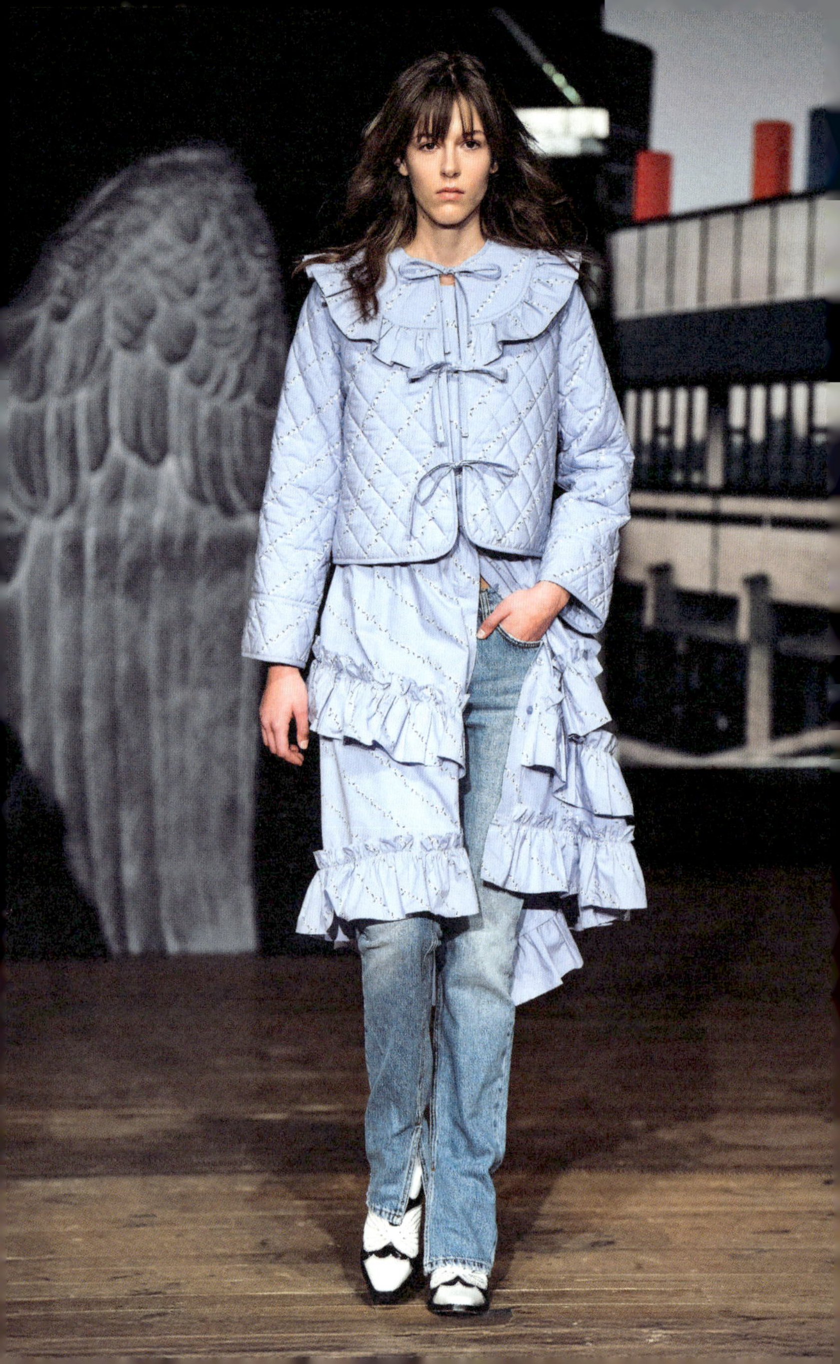

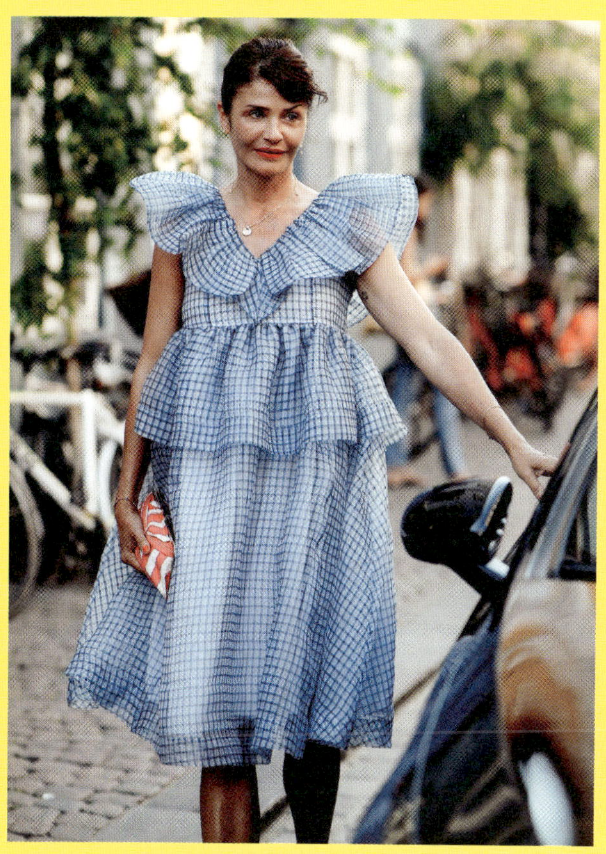

Opposite: A model walks the runway for Ganni at Copenhagen Fashion Week in February 2018.

Above: Danish supermodel Helena Christensen attends the Ganni Spring/ Summer 2021 show at Copenhagen Fashion Week in August 2020.

Overleaf: The Ganni Spring/Summer 2024 runway featured some of Denmark's most buzzworthy models including Mona Tougaard, Chili Dia and Nina Marker. American plus-size model Paloma Elsesser also took part in the show, representing the label's dedication to more inclusive sizing across its lines.

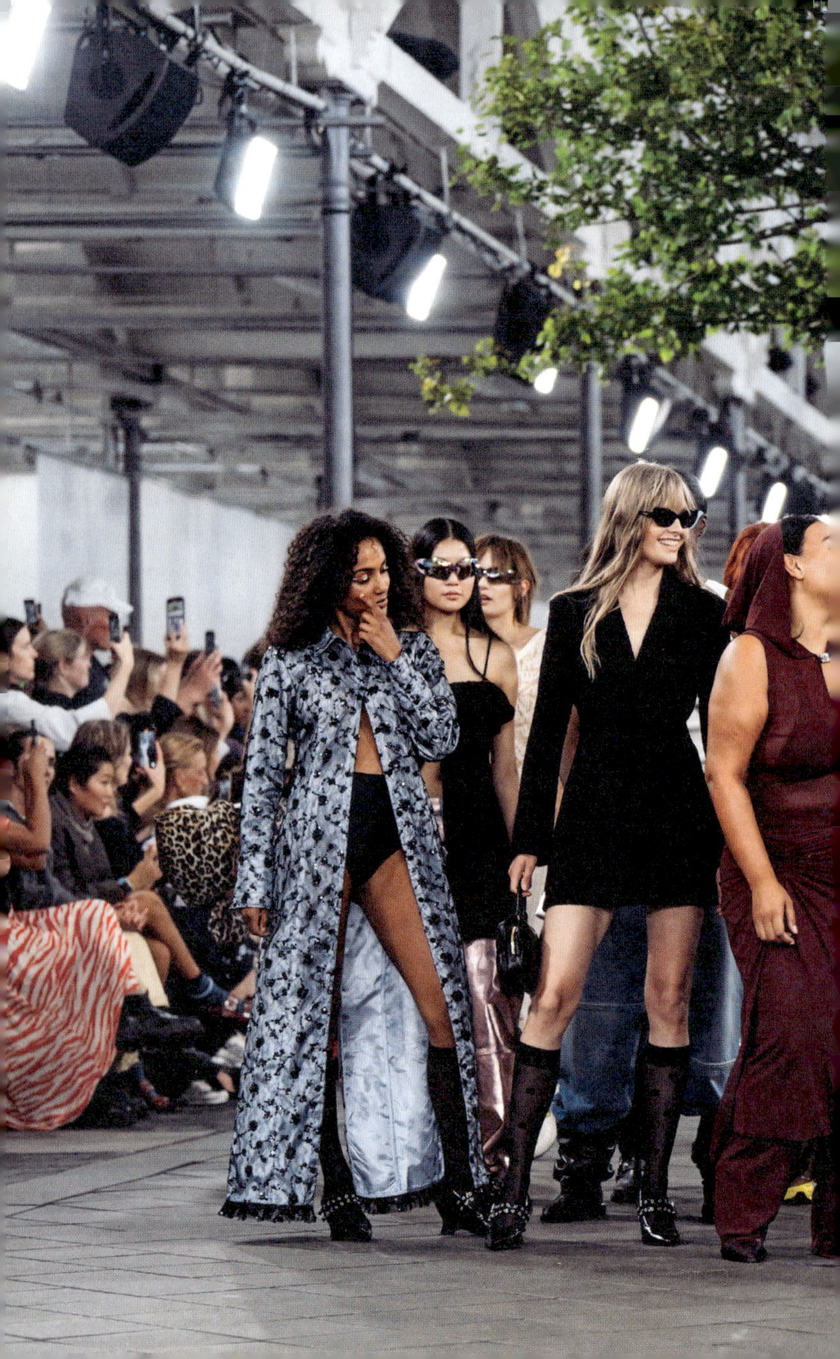

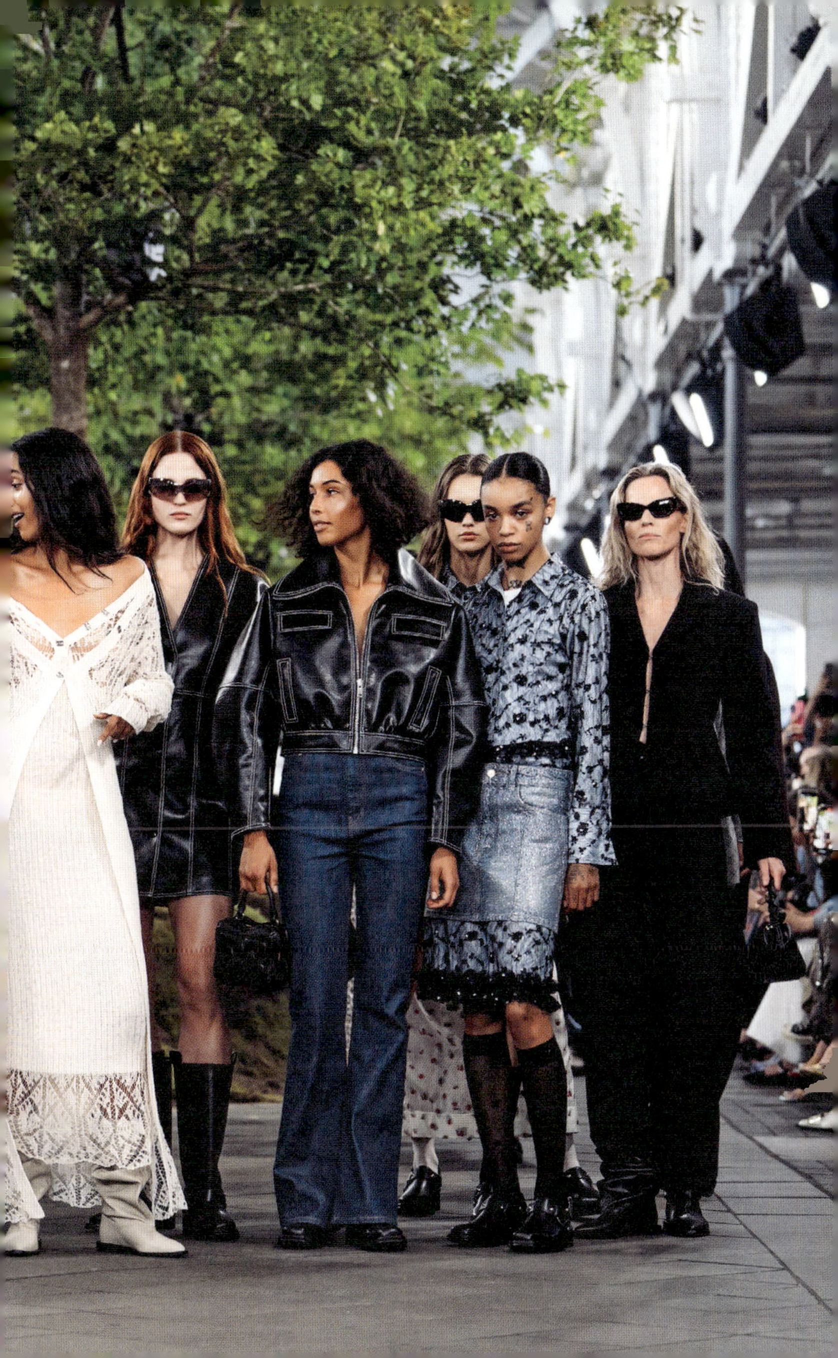

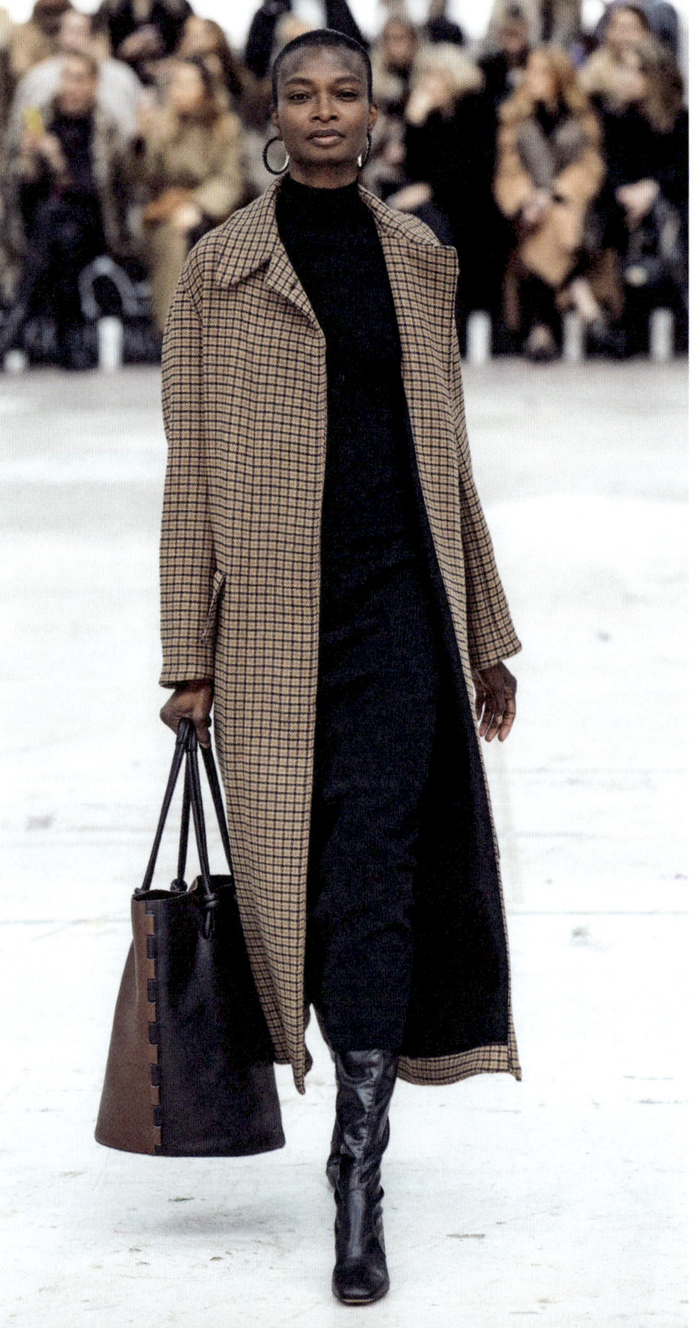

Another key name in bringing Danish fashion to the international stage is none other than Malene Birger. The Copenhagen-born designer graduated from Danish Design School in 2003 and quickly launched her label around the same time. In the following few years, Birger would launch the labels Day Birger et Mikkelsen and By Malene Birger. As Tina Lončar wrote in *Vogue* in 2024:

"The meticulous craftsmanship, thoughtful design, and unwavering commitment to quality in every aspect, along with a focus on comfort and functionality, and time-defying silhouettes, have positioned the Danish brand as a synonym for low-key luxury on the global fashion scene."

Since launching her namesake label in 2006, Stine Goya has become one of the most recognizable Danish labels around. The brand has attracted attention for championing bright, bold colourways and prints paired with whimsical shapes, and flowing cuts. Though obtaining her degree at London's Central Saint Martins, Goya still credits her hometown of Copenhagen for being hugely influential on her craft. "The colors of Copenhagen are an endless source of inspiration. From the colored houses to the breathtaking skies on long summer evenings to all of the different museums with the most inspiring exhibitions, I will never get bored of it," she said in a 2022 interview with *Hypebae*.

A model walks the runway for By Malene Birger at Copenhagen Fashion Week in January 2020.

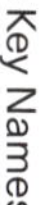

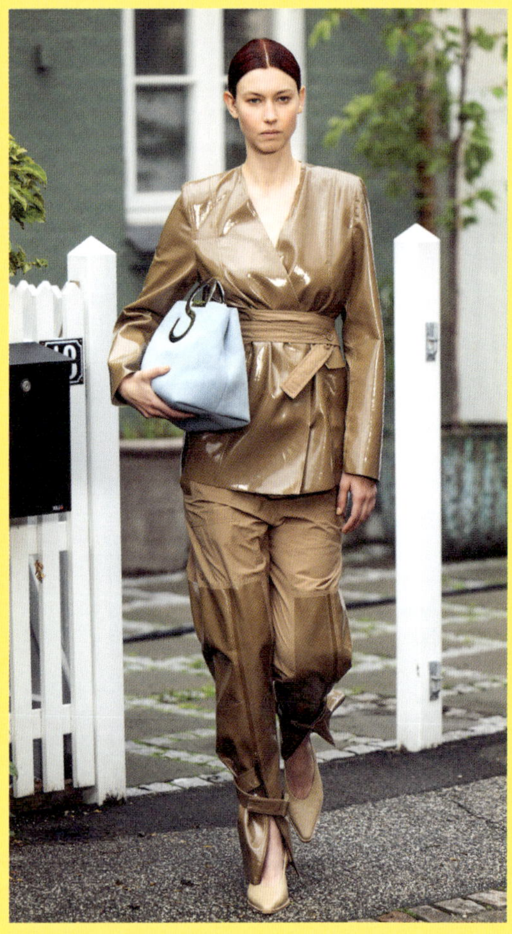

Above: Stine Goya showcased her Spring/Summer 2024 collection (appropriately named "Homecoming") on the very street the Danish designer calls home.

Opposite: Soft colours and feminine cuts are some of Stine Goya's most recognizable features, displayed here in one look from the label's Spring/Summer 2024 collection.

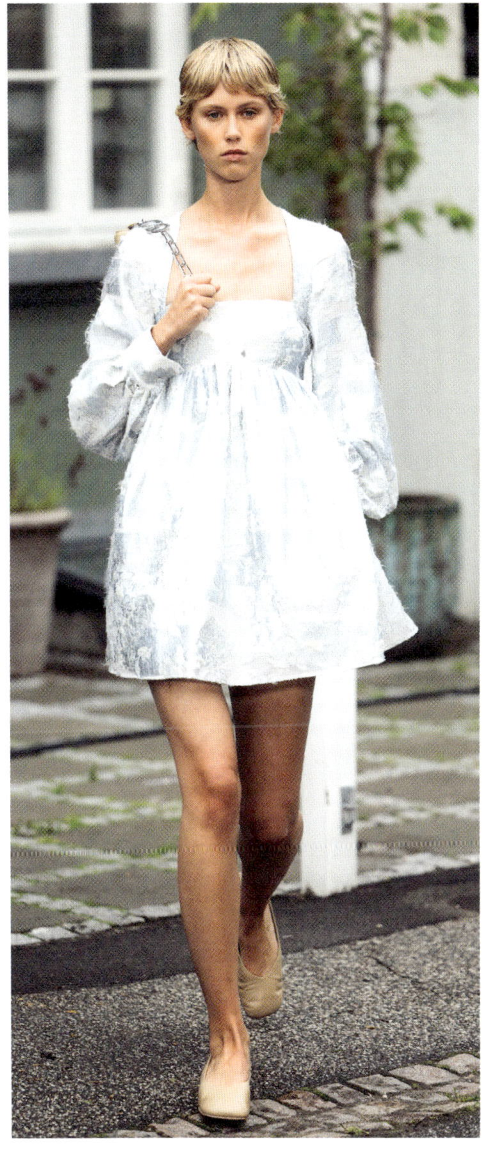

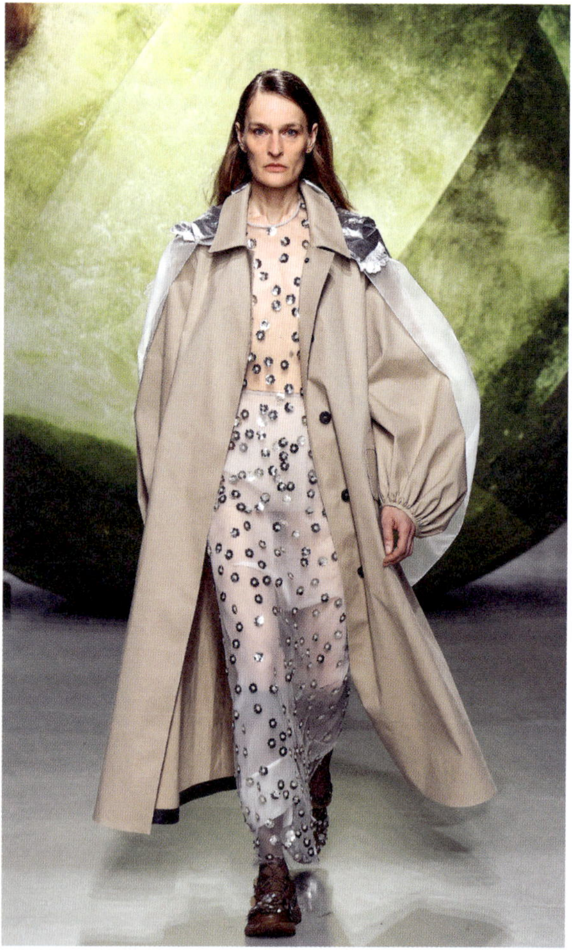

Above: Cecilie Bahnsen's Autumn/Winter 2024 collection was described by the label as emitting "affection and passion", one of the line's looks featured on the runway at Paris Fashion Week in February 2024.

Opposite: A model walks the runway for the Cecilie Bahnsen Autumn/ Winter 2024 show during Paris Fashion Week in February 2024.

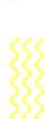

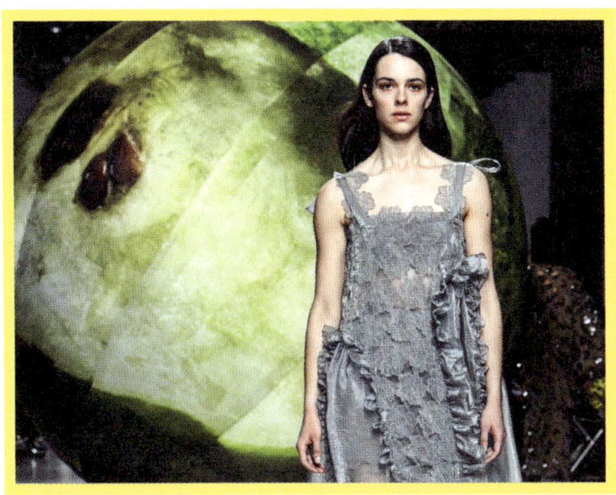

Cecilie Bahnsen has been credited by *Harper's Bazaar* as "the designer behind fashion's prettiest dresses" and had her pieces described as "fantastical, dreamlike wares" by *Vogue*. The ethereal styles have lined the closets of fashion week regulars since the namesake label launched in 2015, and the brand continues to reign as one of Denmark's finest fashion exports for dress-lovers around the world. Bahnsen infuses Parisian notes picked up from her time working under John Galliano with Scandinavian sensibility for silhouettes that bring pretty playfulness into everyday dressing. As Bahnsen told *Forbes* in 2020:

"The beauty of Danish fashion is that everyone is different from one another. It's really not one thing. For a long time, it was really minimalistic, but now everyone is turning that over its head and trying to think outside of the box."

STREETWEAR STAPLES

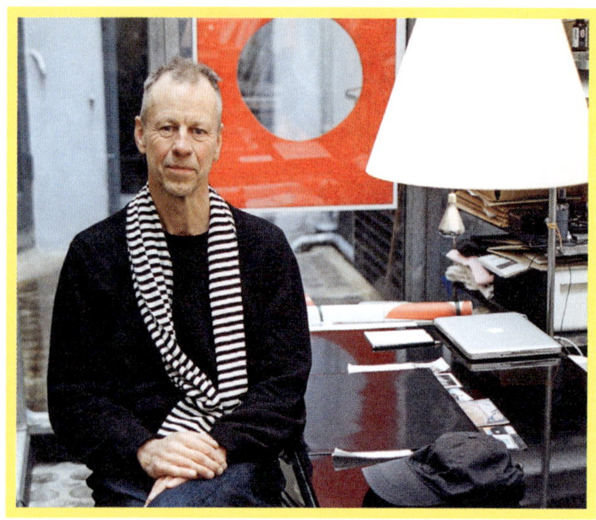

Though technically not established as a brand until the 1980s, the story of Mads Nørgaard and its impact on Copenhagen dates back to 1944 when his grandfather opened a shop in the city centre under the name Sørgemagasinet.

Mads's father, Jørgen, took over the shop in 1958 and would turn it into a key destinations through the 1960s and 1970s. Though Jørgen's legacy can still be seen today, notably through the 101 shirt, an iconic piece released in 1967, Mads's designs have garnered great respect from both Scandinavian and international audiences. His pillow bags and logo beanies are both staples for many Copenhageners.

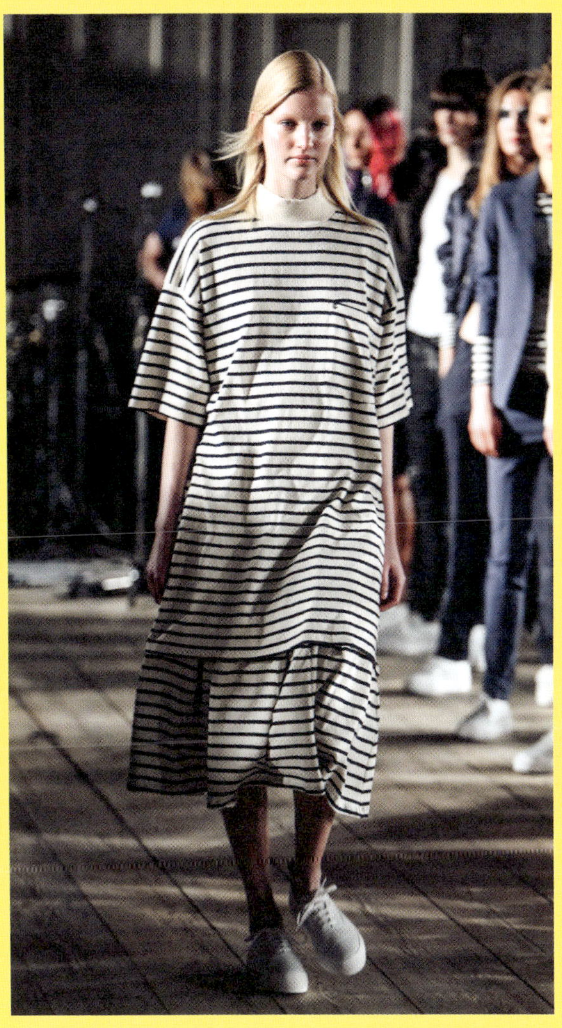

Opposite: Mads Nørgaard pictured in his Copenhagen studio.

Above: A model walks the Mads Nørgaard runway at Copenhagen Fashion Week in January 2014.

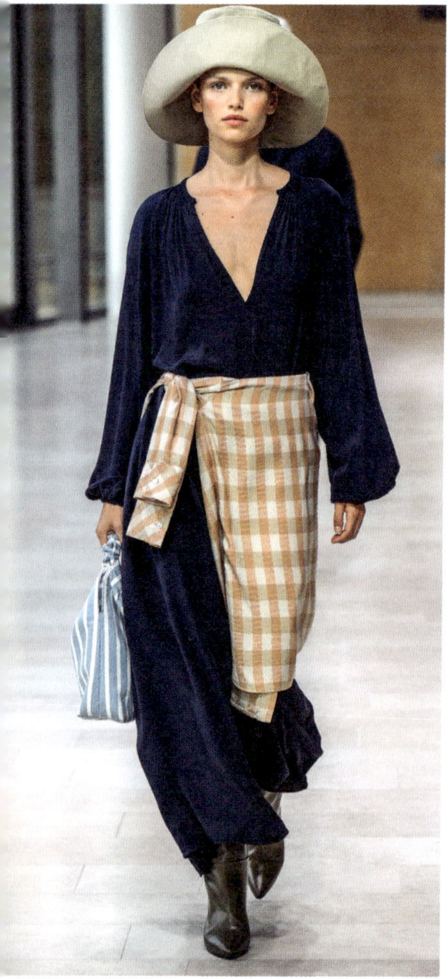

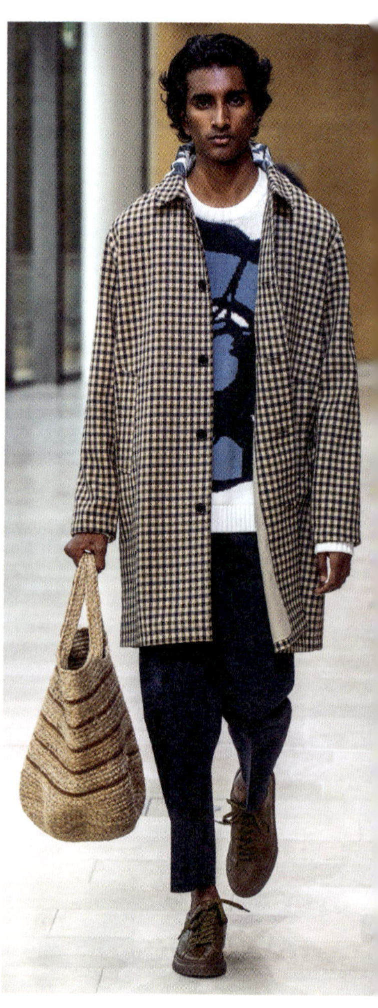

Models walk the Samsøe Samsøe runway at Copenhagen Fashion Week in August 2019.

"Our ideal is democratic, approachable and graceful, with a simple-living, Copenhagen edge to it," Samsøe Samsøe co-founder Peter Sextus remarked in a 2016 interview with *Highsnobiety*. Fans of the label will know that though the brand has evolved in the years since this comment, the sentiment remains the same. Since 1993, the label has acted as a fundamental pillar in Danish fashion – epitomizing much of what the world associates with the nation's aesthetic. Samsøe Samsøe's minimalist approach offered a refreshing take on high-street style for the sartorially inclined, winning the brand placements in some of the world's most respected shopping destinations including London's Carnaby Street and luxury online retailer SSENSE.

In 2002, another name appeared on the Copenhagen scene that would make a big impact for decades to come. Founded by friends Karl-Oskar Olsen and Brian SS Jensen, Wood Wood offered a new approach to dressing that blended premium fashion codes with streetwear styles in a way that wasn't widely accessible in Denmark at the time. This fresh take was welcomed by many of Copenhagen's best dressed and quickly spread internationally with the label becoming a bestseller in New York's Kith store and London's END retailer.

Sunflower came to the fore in 2018 with a focus on fit and quality while maintaining a playfulness that had some comparing the label to Sweden's Acne Studios. "Sunflower is about true classics but with a twist – we like to play around with shapes," Ulrik Pedersen, co-founder of the Danish menswear label, remarked in a 2022 interview with *nss magazine*. Like all good Danish brands, Sunflower creates clothes meant to be worn: "Design plays an important role of course, but when we create a pair of jeans, we are interested in seeing how it will be worn by the people who are part of this group."

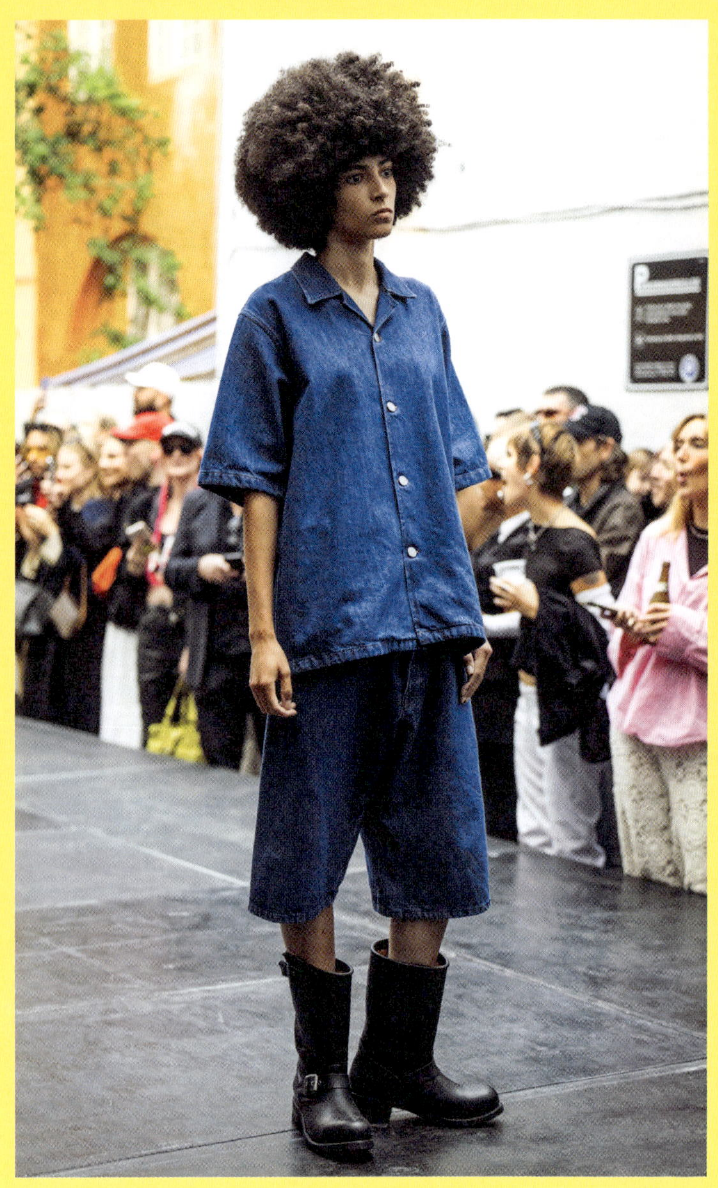

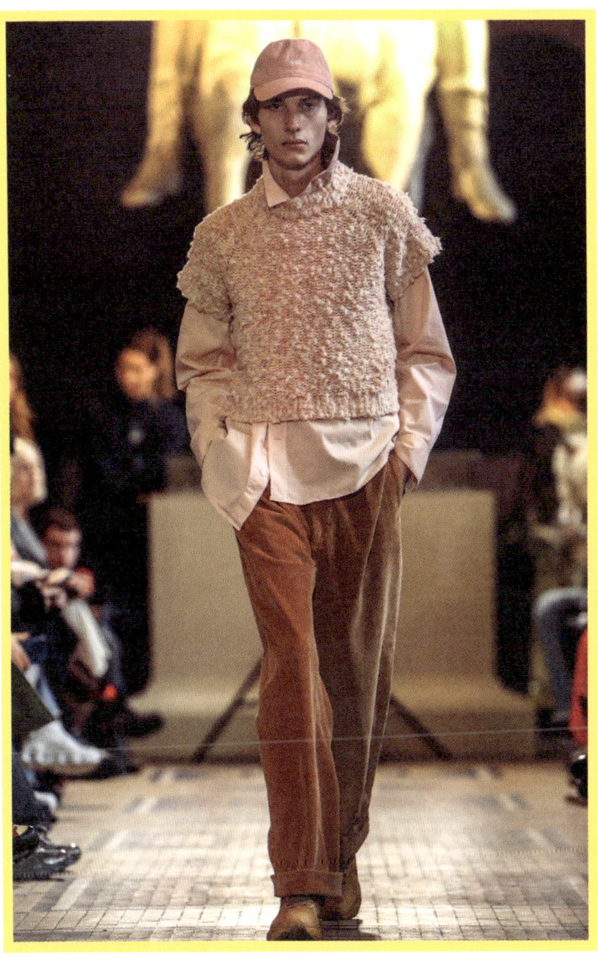

Opposite: Sunflower's love for denim goes beyond just jeans, demonstrated here with the label's Spring/Summer 2024 collection.

Above: A model wears a dusty pink top and hat with corduroy trousers at the Wood Wood runway show as a part of Copenhagen Fashion Week in January 2024.

INDIE ESSENTIALS

Hans Christian Andersen, her artist grandmother and good old-fashioned intuition – these are just a few things that designer Emilie Helmstedt notes as inspirations behind the collections for her namesake label Helmstedt.

"It's about taking your dreams into real life, it's about imagination. For me, it's about being in another world," she said in a 2019 *Vogue* article. Across the seasons, the young designer's love for prints is evident: her signature motif being a handprint from the designer herself. Helmstedt's fantastical yet casual designs have earned the brand a spot in many of Copenhagen's best-dressed residents' wardrobes. The designer is dedicated to using more eco-conscious materials like organic cotton and recycled polyester. In that sense, referring to the label as "a space where art meets fashion and sustainability", as Clara Ferrati of *NSS Magazine* wrote in 2020, seems wholly appropriate.

Caroline Bille Brahe, founder of Caro Editions, described her vision to *Harper's Bazaar* as "beautiful clothing for real people that is playful and easy to wear". Just two years after the brand's inception, the label's Rosie Hair Clip took

Helmstedt's whimsical approach comes to life on the catwalk at Copenhagen Fashion Week for the Autumn/Winter 2024 season.

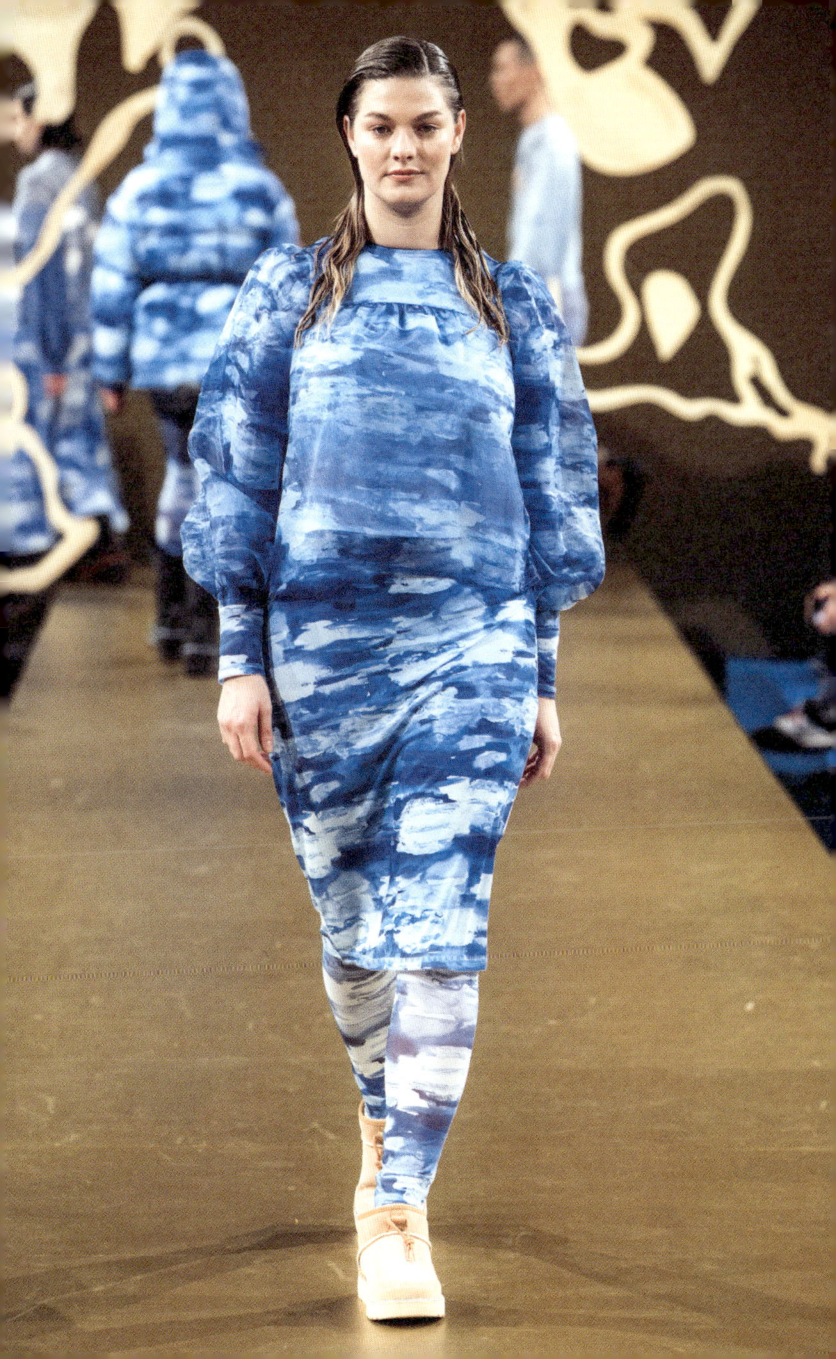

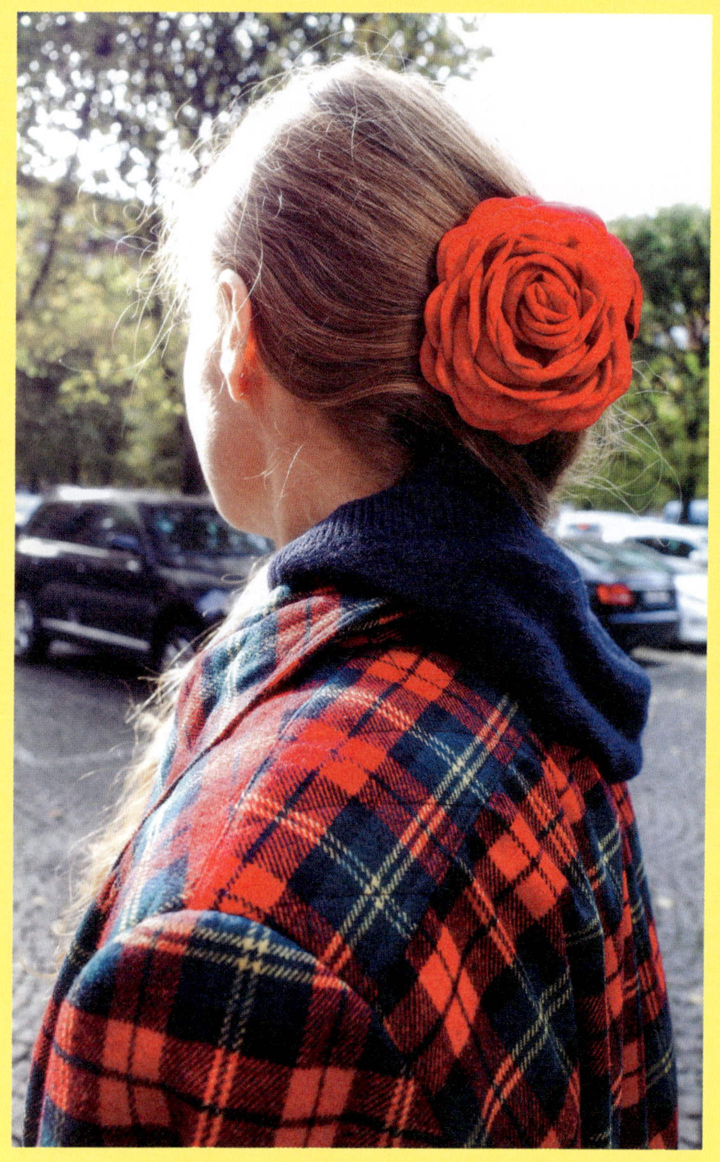

Instagram by storm in 2024 – styled in the hair and on the handbags of some of the app's most admired dressers. Garments by Caro Editions exude a softened 80s-inspired feel with exaggerated cuts and charming details like frill trims or jewel embellishments. However, wearability is never sacrificed. Derived from someone who proudly describes their personal wardrobe as being free from black ("It's a messy colour explosion in a very chic way," Bille Brahe told *Matches Fashion* in a 2022 interview), you can expect a rainbow of colourways on offer from every Caro Editions drop. Though Bille Brahe admitted to *Harper's Bazaar* to having a complicated relationship with the "Scandi girl" label, she also admits that it has its benefits. "There is an ease about Danish style – maybe the attitude as much as the look. Danish women are confident dressers, mixing and matching colors." Caro Editions certainly does a wonderful job of bringing that vibe to the wardrobes of those close to home and further afield.

Skall Studio was founded in 2014 by Julie and Marie Skall, who come from Denmark's Jutland region. Now based in Copenhagen, the sisters grew up in a household that valued quality clothing, as their mother made a lot of their clothes herself. That dedication to expert craftsmanship is now woven into everything Skall Studio does – with the label's much-admired knitwear styles being proudly produced in Denmark at one of the last remaining family-run mills in the country. But it doesn't stop at wool – the use of organic cotton and recycled cashmere has helped to gain the label GOTS (Global Organic Textile Standard) certification. Skall Studio's timeless and responsible designs have solidified the label as a favourite for those with an affinity for clean and understated aesthetics.

Caro Editions' Rosie Hair Clip can be seen in the hair or clipped to the bags of some of Copenhagen's best-dressed residents.

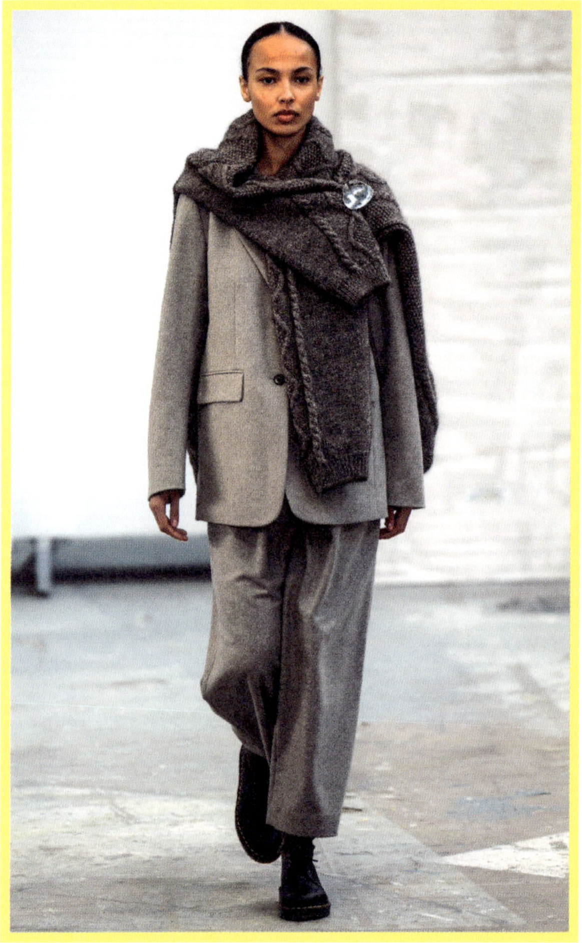

Above: Skall Studio showcases the label's knitwear offering through its Autumn/Winter 2024 collection, presented here in January 2024 at Copenhagen Fashion Week.

Opposite: At the Autumn/Winter 2024 edition of Copenhagen Fashion Week in January 2024, a model walks the runway for Skall Studio.

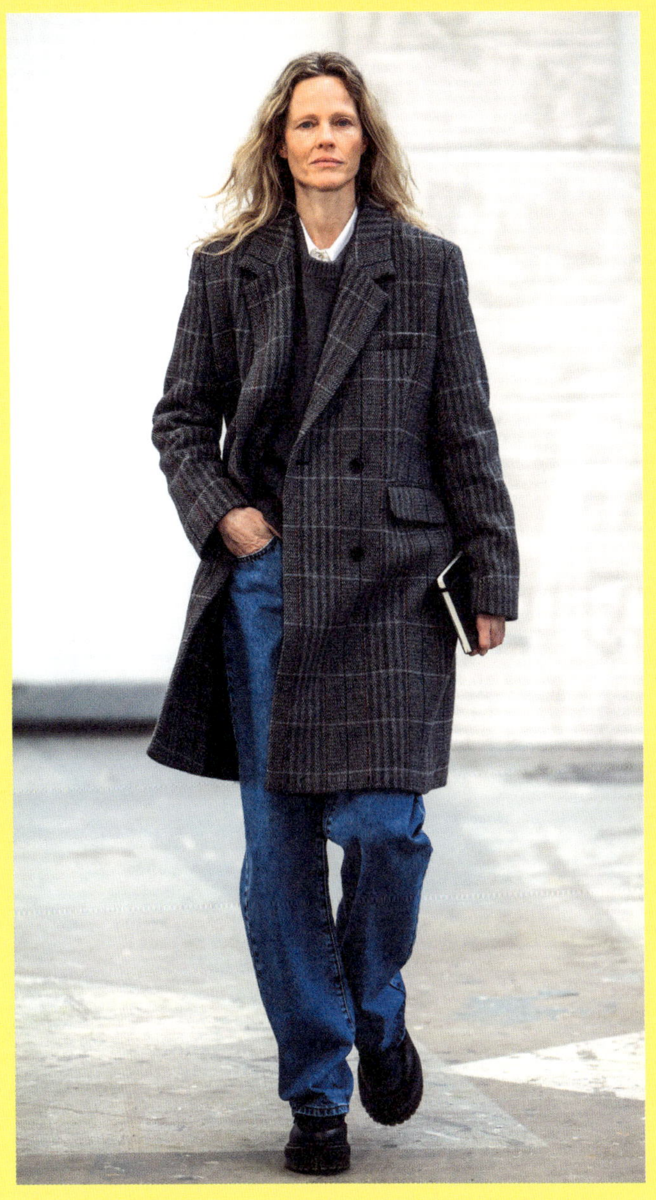

chapter 5

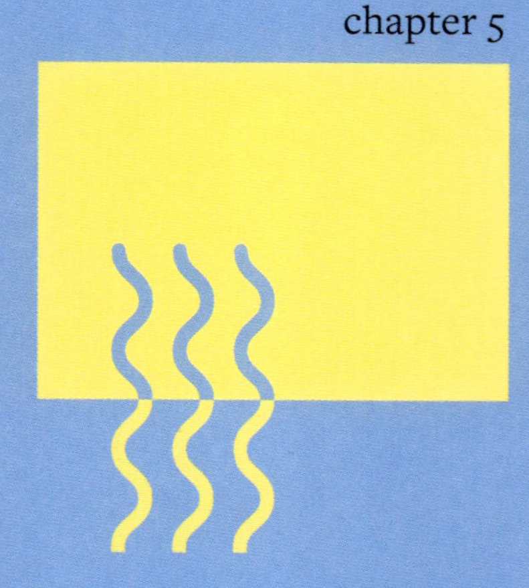

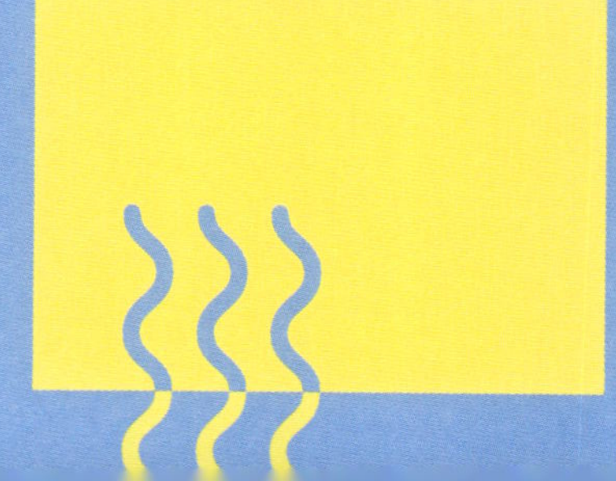

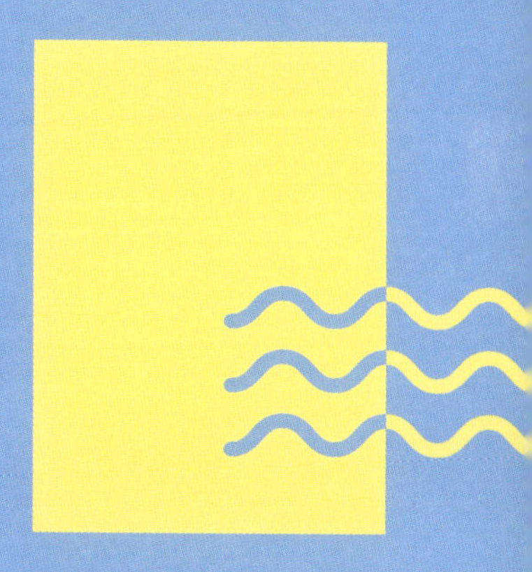

THE CAPITAL OF SUSTAINABILITY

"At a time when the fashion industry is seeking to reverse the environmental damage that it has been contributing to and shift the focus back to slower consumption, the Danes are leading by example. They've set out to create fashion that has the same pure ethos as the mid-century furniture that they've grown up with and been taught to treasure for a lifetime."
***Monocle*, April 2023**

Copenhagen's commitment to being a city that prioritizes environmentally friendly practices isn't anything particularly new – after all, Denmark was the first country in the world to establish a Ministry of Environment and begin developing commercial wind power in the 1970s.

By the 1990s, the movement towards greener practices had gained momentum, and the country has become known for its eco-friendly tourism credentials. Another main factor in Copenhagen topping many "world's most sustainable city" lists is the preferred mode of transport for many residents: the bicycle. Copenhagen boasts an impressive 382 km of cycle lanes across the city, helping approximately 62% of its residents get around every day (yes, many cycle all year round). Cycling is deeply ingrained in the spirit of the Danish capital and proves that, despite the sometimes challenging climate, many Danes are dedicated to keeping their carbon footprint low and appreciating their natural surroundings.

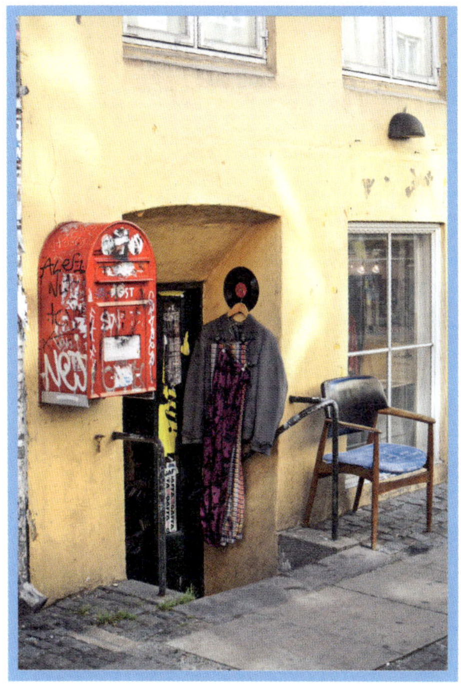

Visitors and locals alike have long praised Copenhagen's selection of second-hand clothing stores.

In the world of food, too, the city has seen a shift towards more sustainable practices (something *The Telegraph* referred to as the "Noma effect") in recent years, with many of the city's Michelin-starred restaurants focusing on organic produce and biodiversity (notably Geranium and The Alchemist). Continuously winning top spots on lists of the world's greenest countries over the past few decades, and with a culture firmly centred around nature and the landscape, it's no wonder that Copenhagen's fashion industry is also a world leader in terms of sustainability.

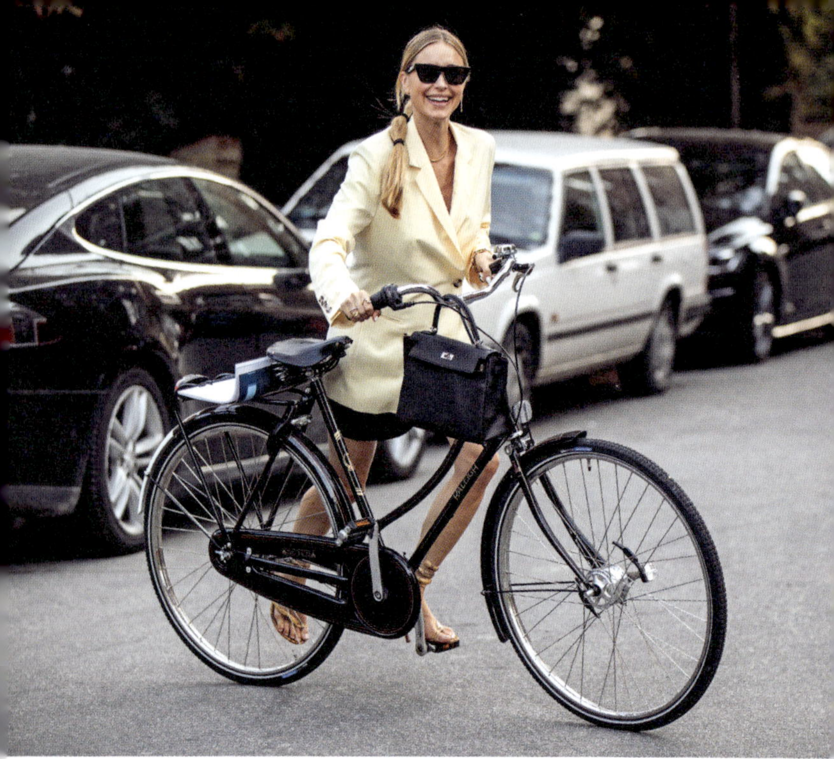

Danish stylist Pernille Teisbaek cycles between shows at Copenhagen Fashion Week in August 2020.

Ganni's creative director Ditte Reffstrup notes that being a Copenhagen-based brand has encouraged the label's interest in sustainable practices, sharing in *InStyle* in 2020: "There's definitely something about living in Copenhagen ... There's the sheer fact that we all cycle. Or we can jump into the harbor and go for a swim. There's a lot of decisions that have been made on a societal level that we take for granted, but it's not necessarily something you see in other places. And I think that definitely plays a role in how the whole fashion, not just the brands, but also the fashion week itself has kind of embraced a sustainability agenda big time."

A VERY GREEN FASHION WEEK

In 2018, Copenhagen Fashion Week welcomed a new CEO who would pioneer more sustainable practices and, in turn, set a new precedent for fashion weeks across the globe. In her first year or so in the new role, Cecilie Thorsmark established a sustainability advisory board and launched a strategy targeting four United Nations sustainable development goals. This led to tangible actions, such as banning single-use plastic bottles and creating a clear guide for more responsible fashion shows. These efforts contribute to Copenhagen's broader objective to achieve carbon neutrality by 2025 and support Denmark's ambitious climate policy to reduce greenhouse gas emissions by 70% compared to 1990 levels by 2030.

Thorsmark has been vocal about the need for systemic change in the fashion industry. "Trends can be fun, but they are not sustainable in any way. There's just something fundamentally broken in the fashion system, and it needs to be fixed," she stated. She advocates for creating long-lasting, high-quality products that are responsibly produced, emphasizing durability and timeless design over fleeting trends.

In 2020, CPHFW took a bold step by making sustainability not just a goal but a strict requirement for the brands it showcases. Thorsmark explained that their sustainability guidelines have transformed their engagement with brands, fostering deeper dialogues with sustainability, production

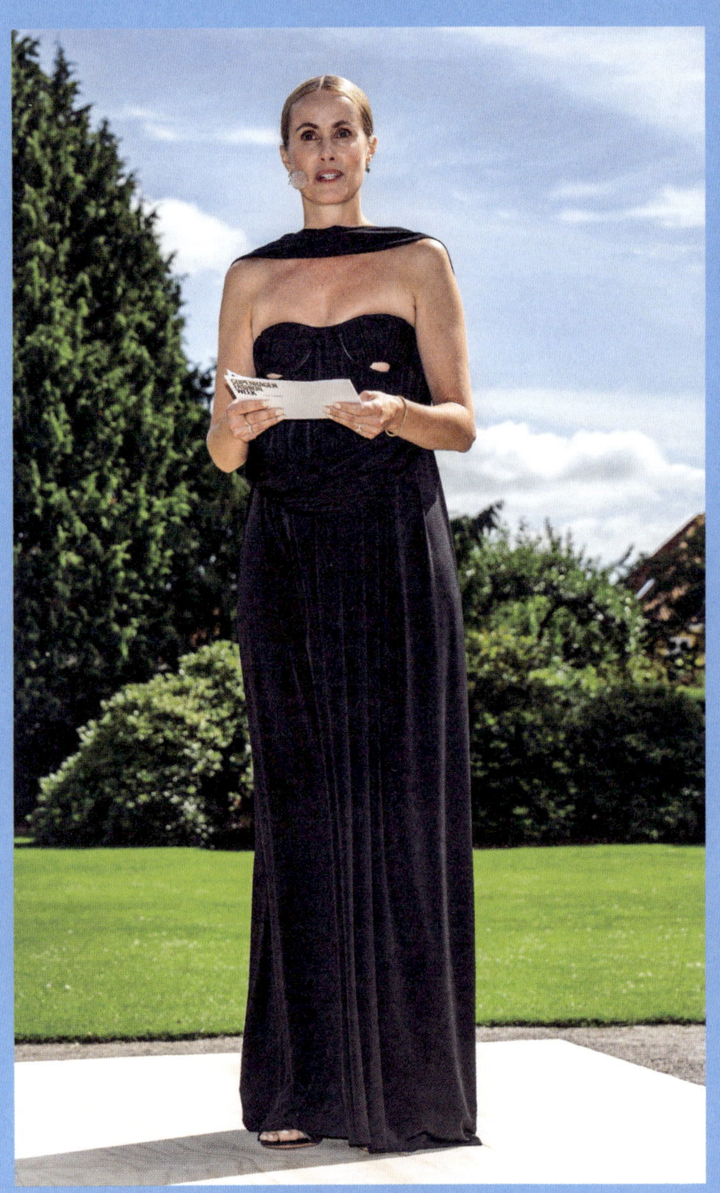

"It is not about if and why sustainability is important but how to implement measures with the greatest impact on environmental and social sustainability. More and more brands are aware of their material and design choices and of course, we see more designs made of already existing materials be it in the form of deadstock, reuse, or recycling."
Cecilie Thorsmark

and buying teams. This ongoing interaction has provided CPHFW with valuable insights into the daily operations of brands, helping to identify both challenges and opportunities in sustainability.

Though some of Copenhagen's sustainability credentials align naturally with Danish culture (for example, bike lanes have existed in the city since the early twentieth century and have evolved with the city rather than being an intentional addition for the sake of greener transport), one of the latest moves towards more eco-friendly standards would go against the city's roots. In 2022, CPHFW announced that it would be the first global fashion week to go fur-free. This would come after years of Denmark operating as a big exporter of mink fur, used mainly in the garment industry. By choosing to go against what many would consider a vital component of Danish fashion, it's clear that the commitment to a greener future is strong.

Chief executive of Copenhagen Fashion Week Cecilie Thorsmark speaks during the Copenhagen Fashion Week SS25.

SETTING A SUSTAINABLE STANDARD

"All the scientists you can fit into a room will say the same thing, and it's that fashion brands need to make less. There's too much production going on."
Malene Birger, Chief Executive, Morten Linnet

Beyond Copenhagen's talent for birthing brands that produce some of the nicest-looking clothing, the city has also proved to have a penchant for fostering labels that have tipped the world of sustainability on its head.

There are a host of Danish brands that have surfaced over the last few years that have done an incredible job of smashing any preconceived notions regarding eco-friendly practices needing to have a particular aesthetic. A prime example of this is the sibling-owned label (di)vision. Since 2018, Nanna and Simon Wick have focused their designs around deadstock fabrics. Simon told *V* magazine in 2022,"Working with deadstock fabrics gives a more unpredictable touch to the brand. When we design a collection, we don't know what is available until we source the fabrics." Tablecloths, parachutes and plenty of other second-hand materials have found their way into (di)vision's collections, with the label's first piece

A model sports a patchwork look from (di)vision during Copenhagen Fashion Week Autumn/Winter 2022.

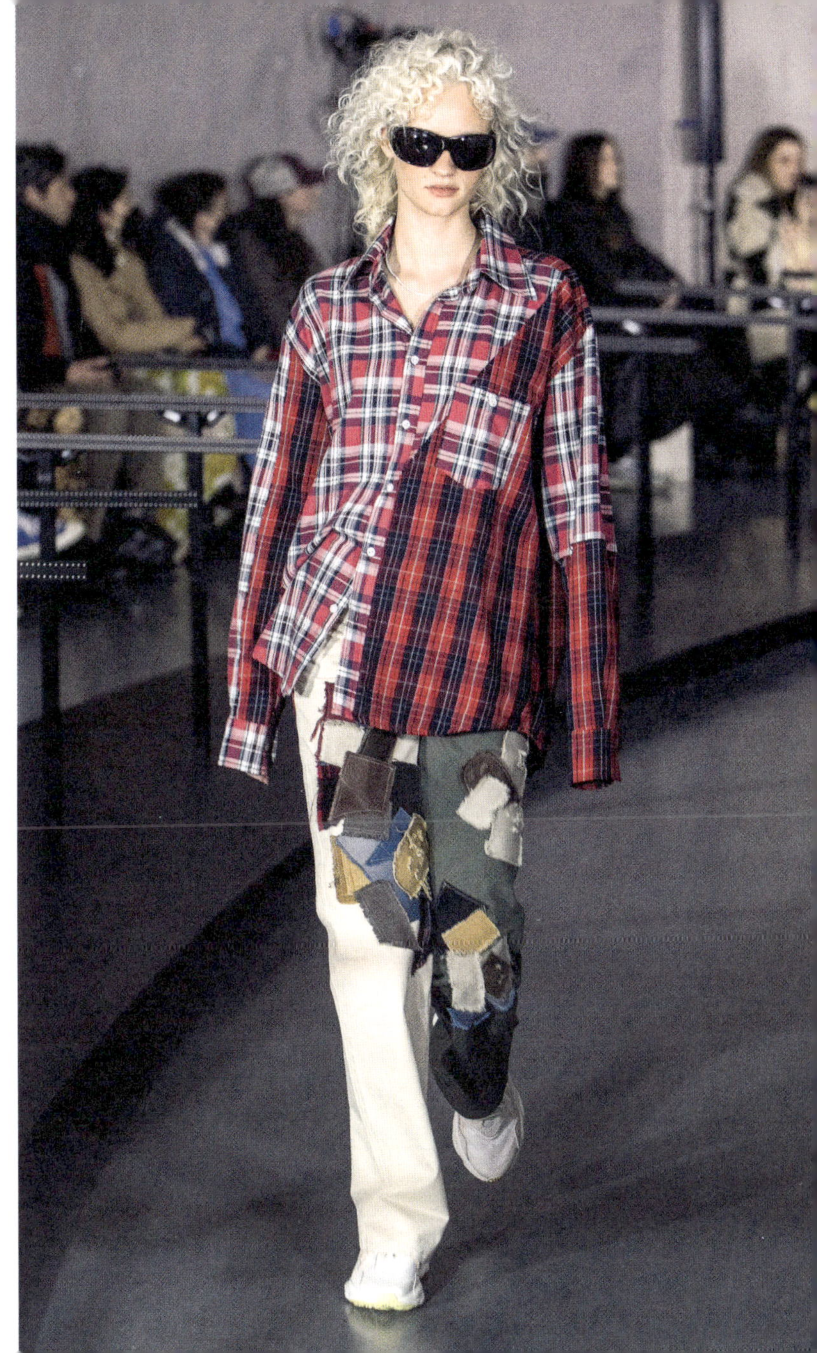

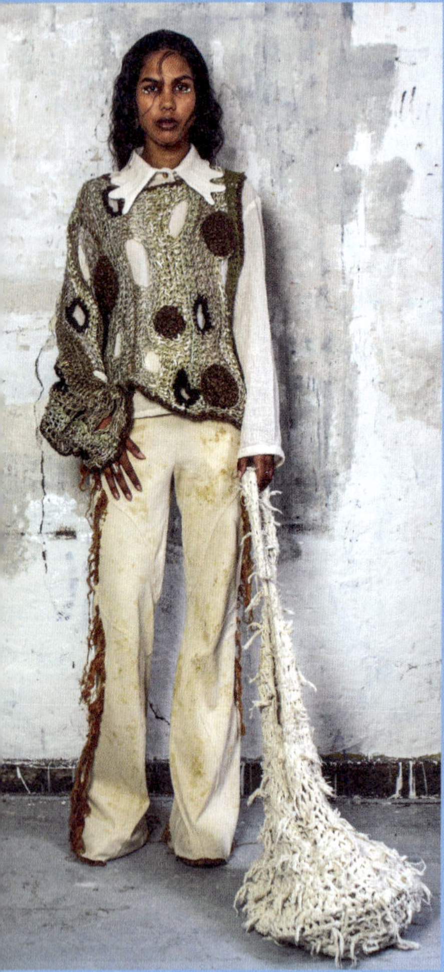

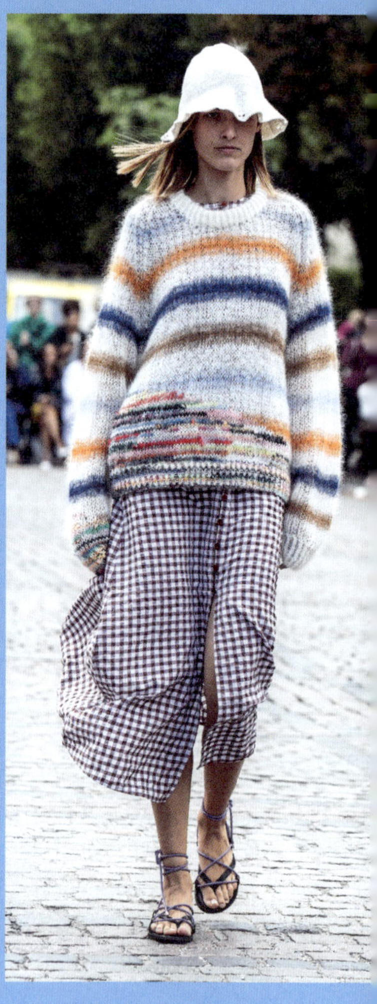

Above left: Solitude Studios look from the label's 2021 "Landscaping" lookbook captured by photographer Erik Andrè Nes.

Above right: Lærke Bagger's collaboration with Soulland graces the runway at Copenhagen Fashion Week in August, 2019.

being a reworked MA-2 bomber jacket made from vintage surplus military gear. The brand has found its own unique groove in terms of aesthetic. *AnOther Magazine* calls it "equal parts glitz and grunge", which co-founder Simon Wick agrees reflects the label's outlook.

Solitude Studios has also played an important role in championing sustainability in the Copenhagen fashion scene – served with a full dose of experimental energy. What do coffee, tea, rust and swamp water have to do with this Danish label? They're all used as dyes in Solitude Studios' designs. "Our use of the local bog to dye our fabrics [gives] something to nature that was initially taken from it, letting it reclaim this piece of itself that has been borrowed and shaped by humans," co-founder Jonas Sayed Gammal Bruun told *Bricks Magazine* in a 2024 interview. Solitude Studios first came to fame in 2020 with its aptly named seaweed bags and has since become a mainstay in the Copenhagen Fashion Week schedule. The label continues to demonstrate its dedication to innovation both in terms of approach and materials, inspiring the *Vogue* headline: "What Is Bogcore? A Trend That Could Only Have Come from Copenhagen."

Another name dedicated to handmade and upcycled pieces is Copenhagen's Lærke Bagger, who started knitting at just age eight. She has become something of a celebrity for her work both in Denmark and abroad. She has built a reputation for encouraging people to reject fast fashion and create their own designs instead. Bagger's CV has proven that upcycling and focusing on sustainable practices doesn't need to limit your reach, having worked alongside Soulland on its Spring/Summer 2020 collection and now proudly dressing clients including Miley Cyrus.

A STYLISH SHIFT

Even labels that may not have set out with clear intentions around sustainability have caught on to the importance of being greener. Co-founder and CEO of Ganni, Nicolaj Reffstrup, told *Vogue Scandinavia* in 2021: "The appetite is there ... now it's time for the fashion industry to wake up to outsourcing clothes." In 2019, the label launched Ganni Repeat, a platform which allows customers to rent Ganni styles. Ganni Repeat has since evolved to allow Ganni customers to resell, recycle and repair both new and pre-loved Ganni pieces.

The creative directors of Baum und Pferdgarten, Rikke Baumgarten and Helle Hestehave, are known to speak out against overconsumption in fashion and are responsible for launching the label's ambitious goals around sustainability. "Each year we evaluate our own performance on numerous parameters and publish a report which we share publicly on our website as we really believe in transparency and honesty is the best way forward," the pair explained in a 2021 interview with *Harper's Bazaar*. The label offers an extensive guide to its production and materials on its website and presents easy how-to videos on making its apparel last as long as possible across its social media accounts.

Models line up for the Baum und Pferdgarten Spring/ Summer 2022 show at Copenhagen Fashion Week.

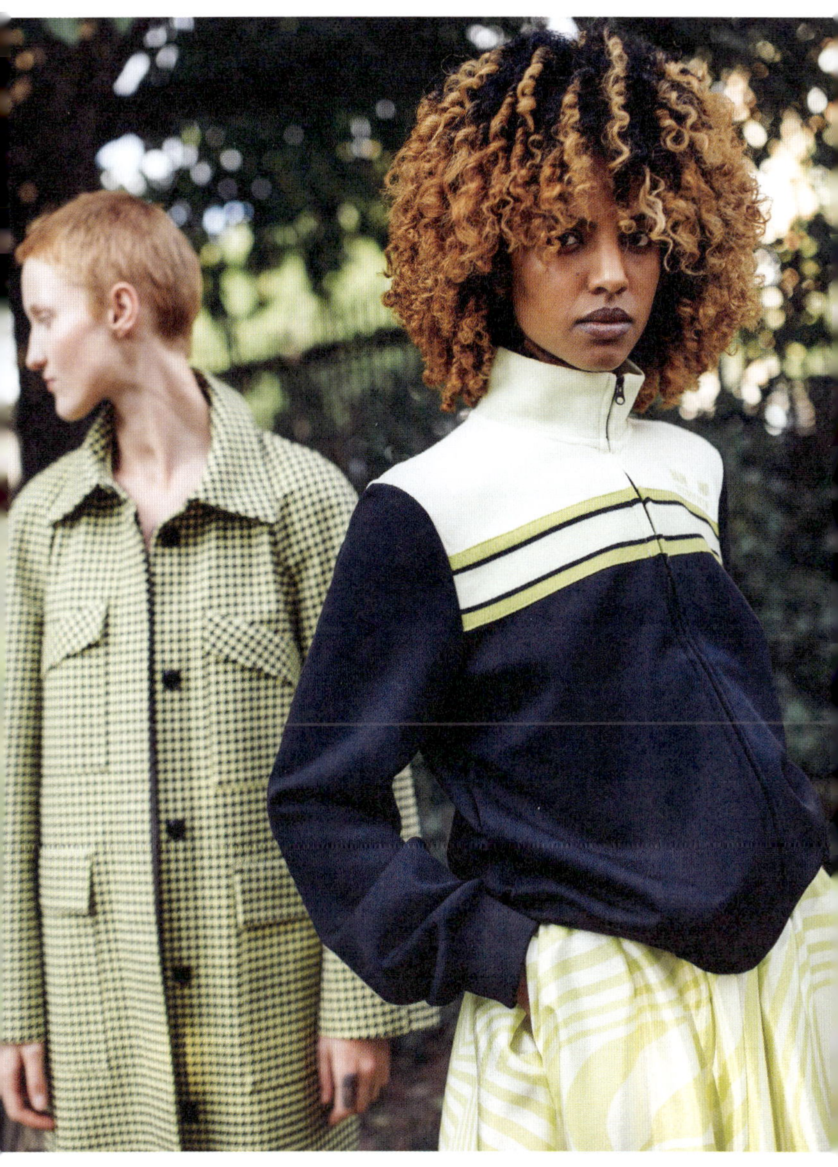

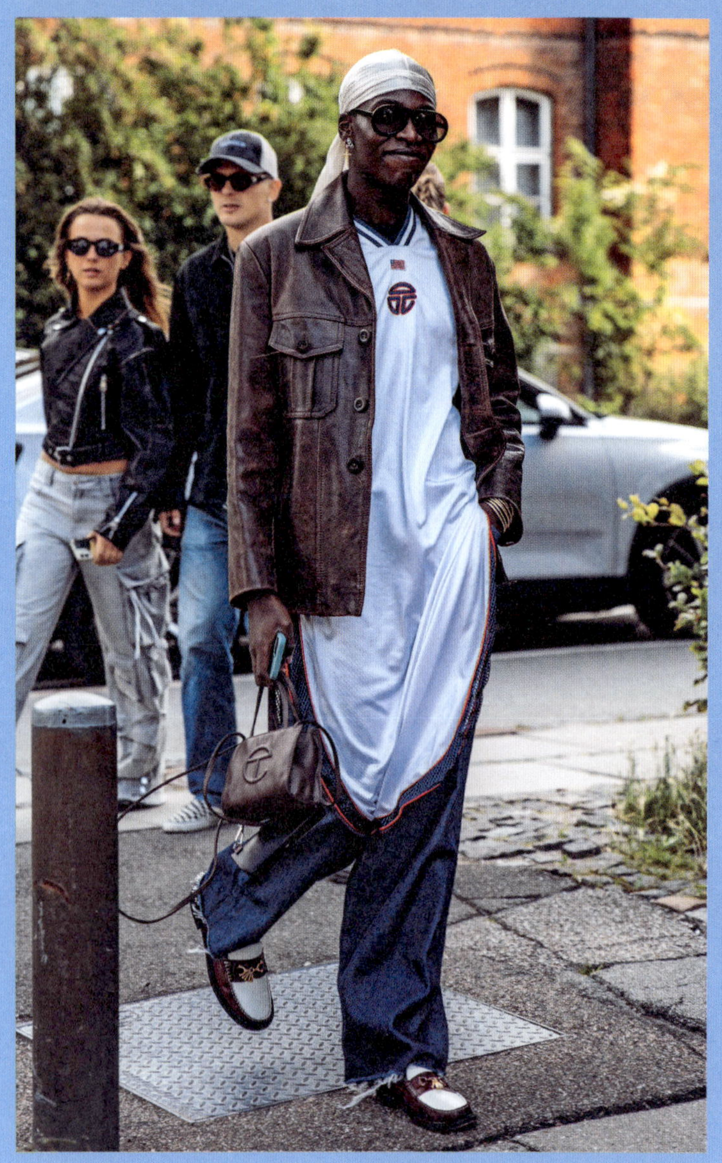

DEDICATION TO SECOND-HAND SHOPPING

From the iconic Time's Up Vintage and Paloma, which specialize in designer pieces from bygone eras, to the curated menswear haven that is BauBau, the Copenhagen second-hand selection is definitely something to write home about (read: come with plenty of room in your suitcase or regret it forever).

But perhaps even better than the vintage clothing shops on offer is Copenhagen's culture of second-hand markets. Known as "Loppemarked", these markets tend to take place on the weekends between April and October and allow sellers to set up stalls laden with second-hand goods. Loppemarked på Bryggen is one of the city's most popular outdoor markets, partially due to its idyllic location on the Islands Brygge quay. Here you can find a broad range of goods ranging from vintage furniture to clothing and toys, making it a destination for many young families. Det Grønne Loppemarked (the green market) has become a firm favourite for young creatives over the past few years, partly due to its location in the Nørrebro neighbourhood. Alongside the stalls of pre-owned clothing and other items, this market proudly hosts a range of local, small-scale food producers as a way to promote greener living. With such a thriving second-hand culture and commitment to community initiatives, it's no wonder that the city inspires some of the most innovative fashion designers in the game.

Apparel rental services play an important part in the environmentally conscious fashion-forward Copenhageners. One such company is Rented, the name behind this look sported by Rodrigue Kitwanga at Copenhagen Fashion Week in 2023.

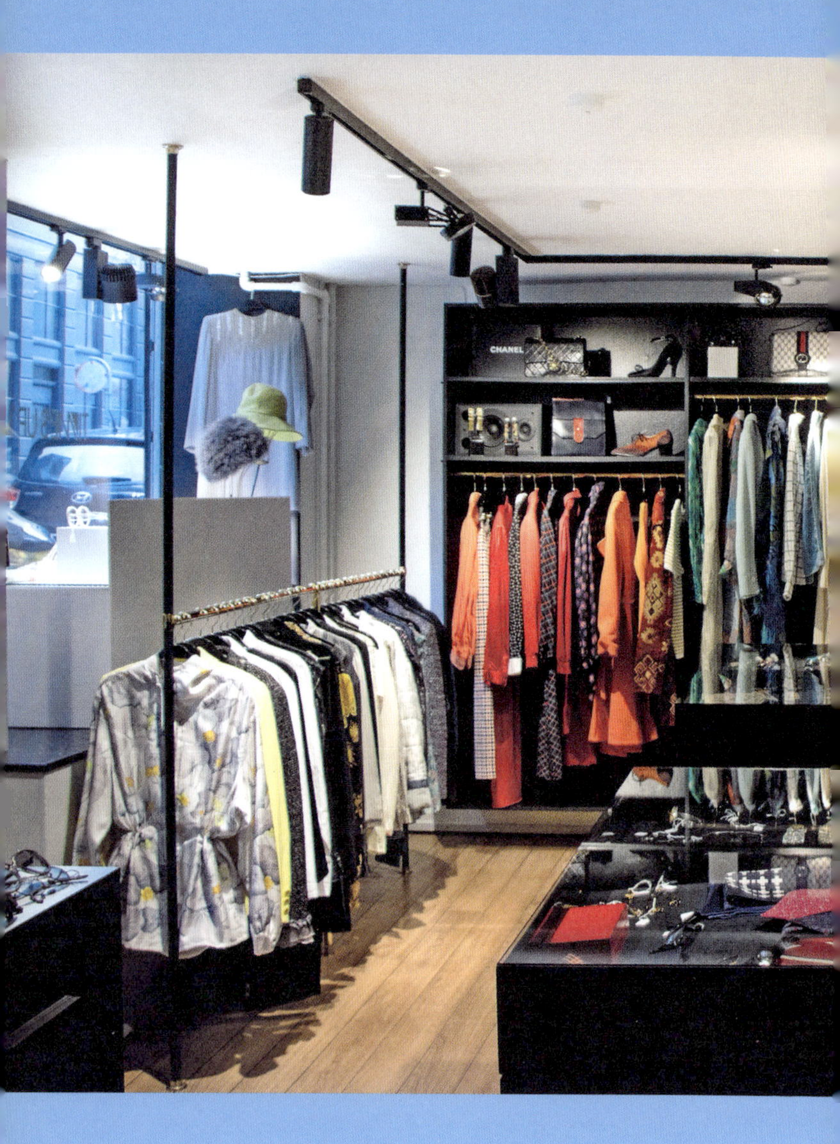
CHANEL

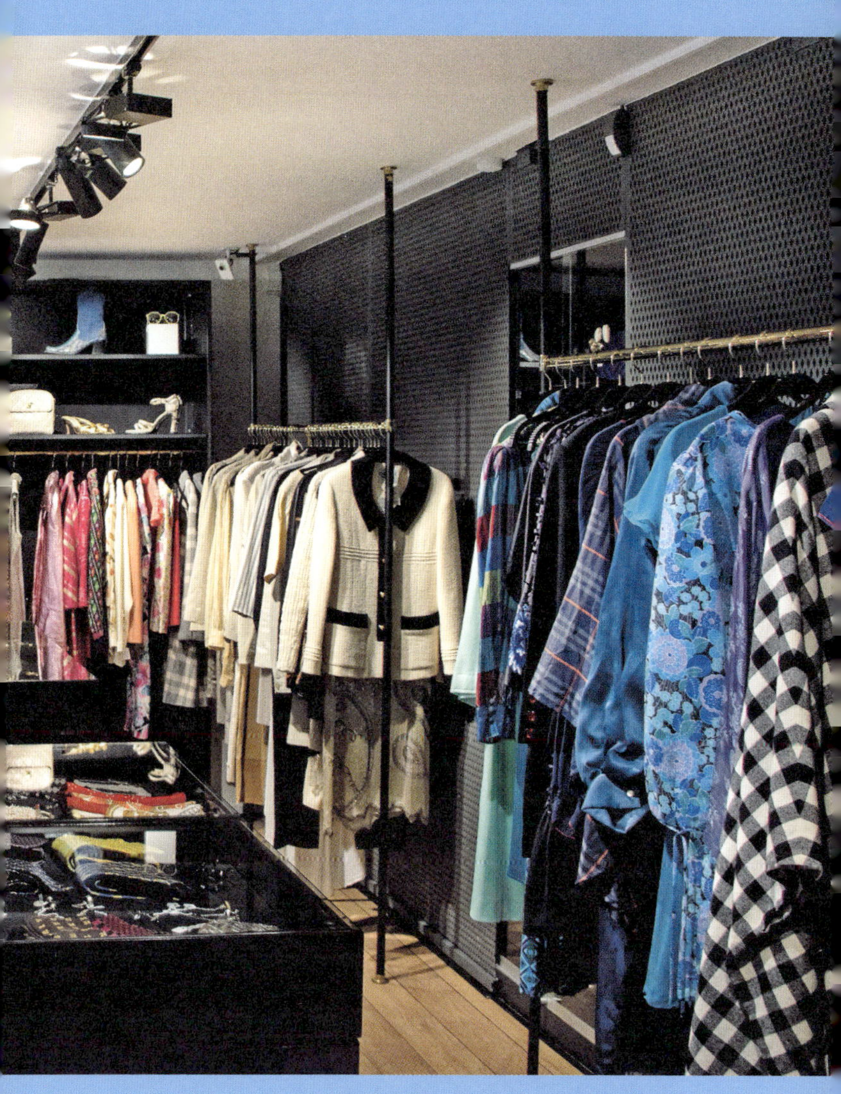

Time's Up Vintage has been serving Copenhagen residents and visitors for over a decade and continues to be a mainstay.

chapter 6

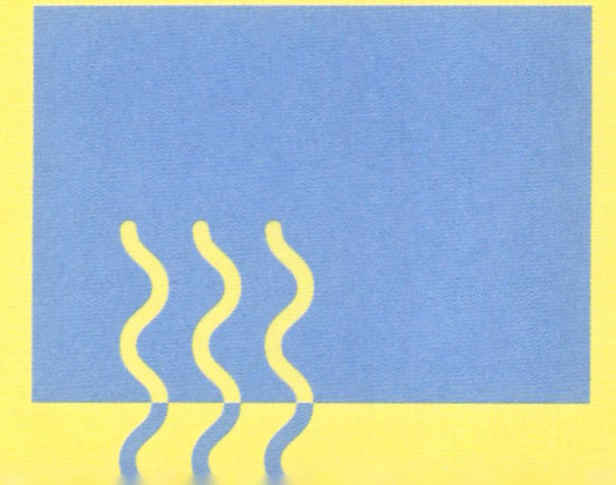

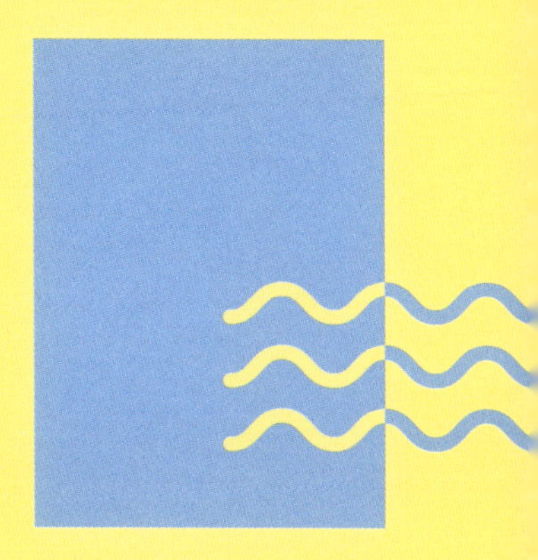

FUTURE PLAYERS

Once synonymous with a bohemian aesthetic and handcrafted charm, Danish fashion has gone through plenty of changes over the years. Now, as the mid-2020s approach, there's a new shift in what it means to be a Danish apparel brand or designer – as subversion increasingly takes centre stage at Copenhagen Fashion Week. Behind this transition are a few key names that dominate the spotlight, propelling Denmark forward as a nation that champions innovation and experimentation. Here's an insight into a few of these creative masterminds to better understand where exactly Danish fashion is heading.

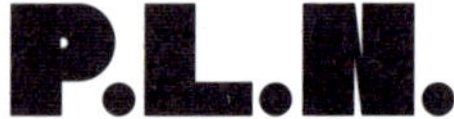

Peter Lundvald Nielsen launched his namesake label P.L.N. in 2020 – a dark year for many around the world. However, this seemed to be quite fitting. *Paper Magazine* spoke about Nielsen in a 2022 piece: "The designer brings a dark, gritty energy to his clothes, which exude a raw, almost industrial quality. Most of his pieces are upcycled, and all of them are black. If that aesthetic seems at odds with Copenhagen's image of carefree, happy bohemia, well, that's sort of the point."

UK techno, 1990s American skate culture and even religious attire serve as inspiration for P.L.N. collections, presented at Copenhagen Fashion Week via unforgettable immersive experiences that continually captivate and inspire ("Nielsen's assembled troupe trudged out like characters from a particularly dark fantasy RPG," one Dazed Magazine journalist wrote about the SS23 runway show). If you're imagining a scene where you might find Kanye West in an all-black ensemble, you're on the mark. The rapper is known to be a fan of the brand, sporting a hat from them during his surprise 2022 appearance at the BET Awards.

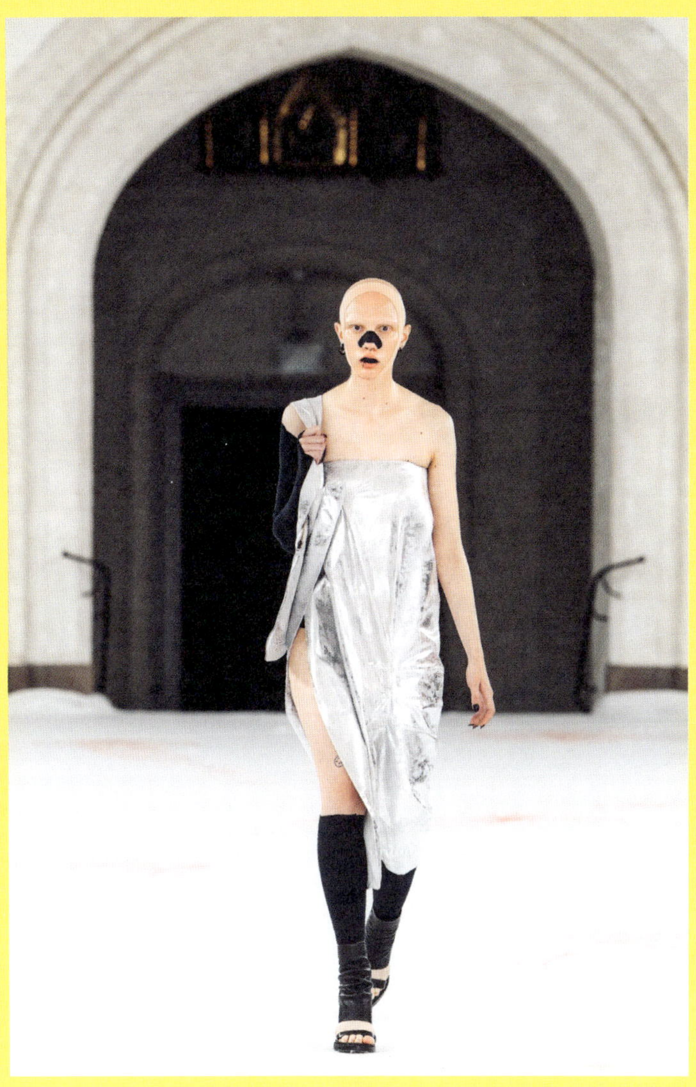

P.L.N.'s Spring/Summer 2024 show took place in Nikolaj Kunsthal, an old church-turned-gallery in central Copenhagen.

NICKLAS SKOVGAARD

Nicklas Skovgaard's dedication to experimenting with craftsmanship has gained the young designer respect from fashion lovers worldwide. "The Danish Designer Creates a World of Perverse Whimsy, Driven by His Own Curiosity," reads one headline on Skovgaard's work from luxury retailer SSENSE. If given the chance to witness a Nicklas Skovgaard show at Copenhagen Fashion Week, it will all makes sense. The designer's origin story is about as fantastical as his designs. The protagonist discovered a second-hand children's loom that would inspire him to experiment with different materials and techniques, all while being encouraged by his mother, who would become his first client.

Since officially launching in 2020, the the Nicklas Skovgaard brand has become a favourite of celebrity stylist Harry Lambert, who introduced the label to perennial It girl Alexa Chung. She wore a feathered black micro shorts and crop-top ensemble from the brand on the red carpet at the prestigious Vogue World event in 2023. Skovgaard also rejects traditional formats for his presentations: his SS24 show saw fellow fashion designer and performer Britt Liberg disrobe live for a captivated audience. Vilda Krog of *Office Magazine* remarked on the show: "Skovgaard appears to have transcended temporal boundaries, reminiscent of the semiotic eras overseen by Galliano and McQueen."

Performer Britt Liberg displays Nicklas Skovgaard's designs during Copenhagen Fashion Week in August 2023.

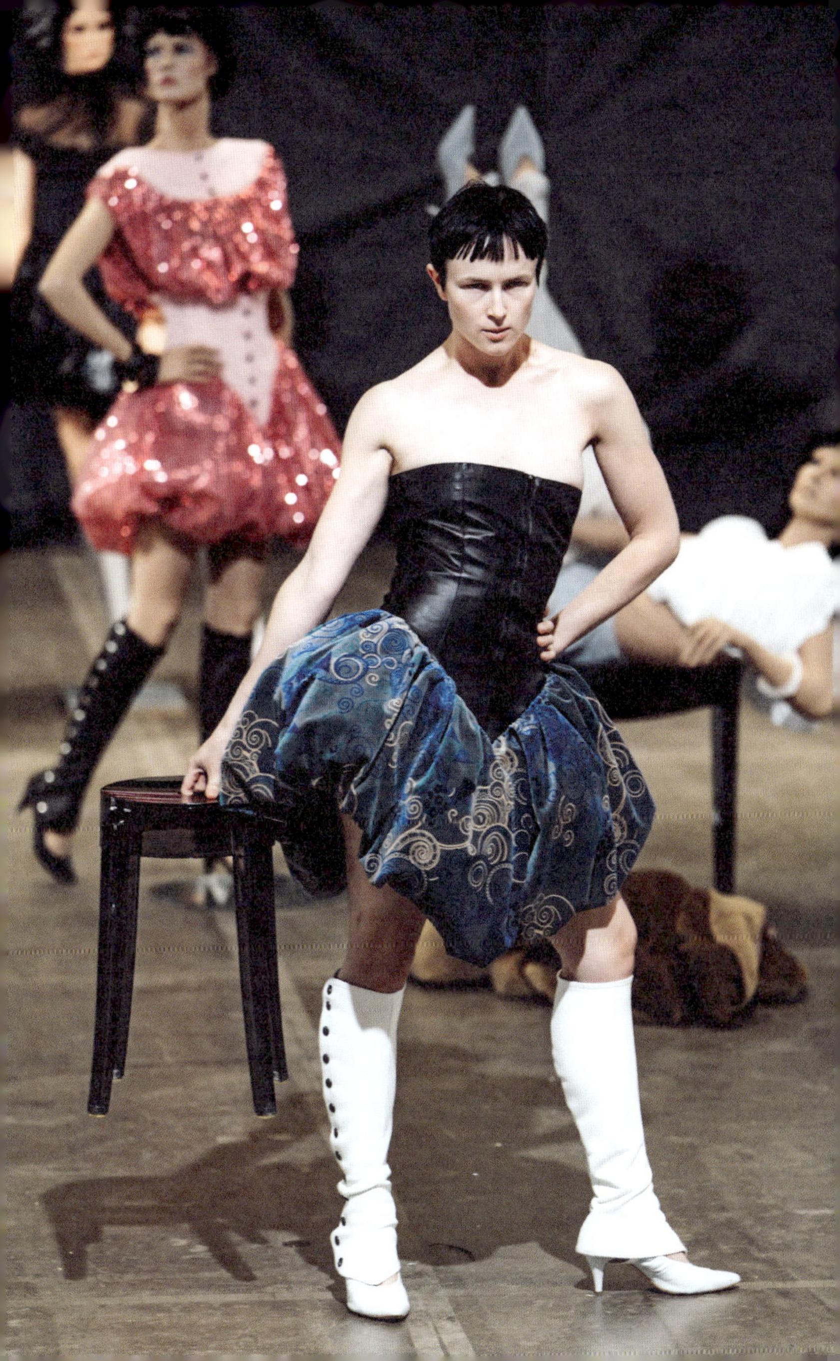

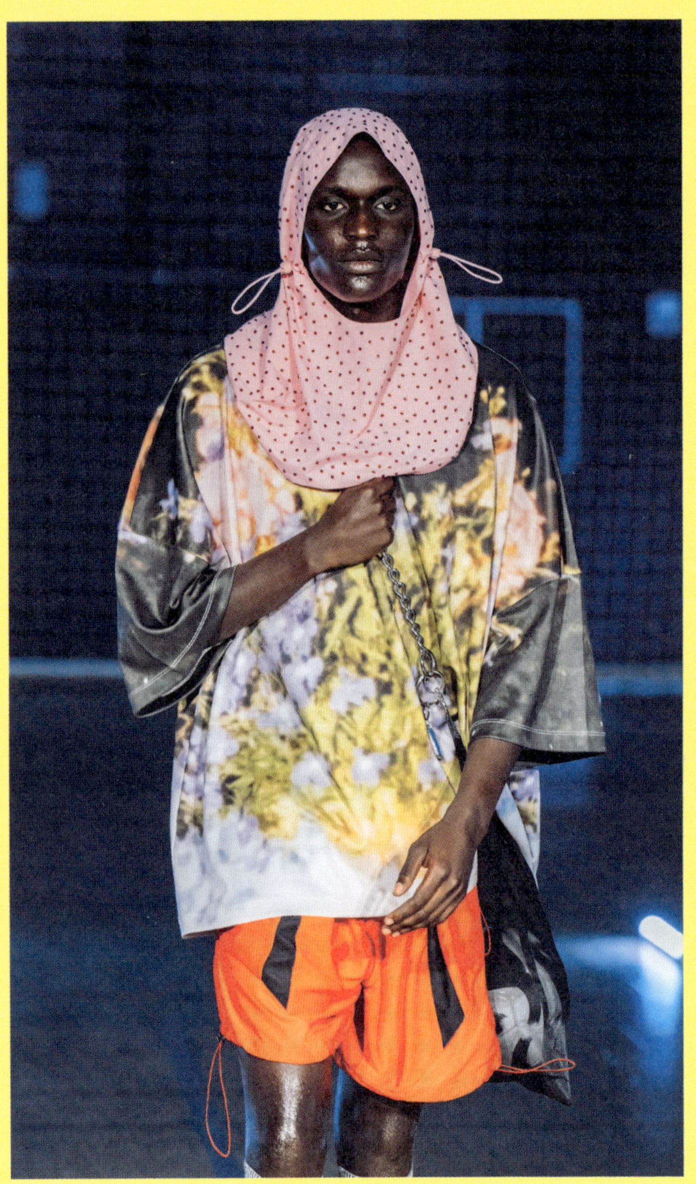

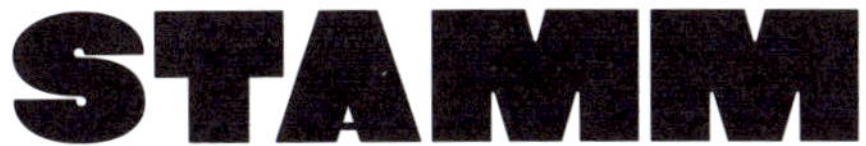

"We always wanted to drive a change, not just in design but also in finding the most beautiful meaning in life when worlds and cultures collide. When we say that we create for longevity, we mean that each design is first and foremost genderless and diverse, using more responsibly sourced materials," Elisabet Stamm remarked in a 2023 interview with *Scandinavian MIND*.

The Danish designer has succeeded in bringing together heavy hip-hop influences with sustainable practices since launching her namesake label in 2022, winning the Zalando Sustainability Award for Fall 2023. As the label moved into its third year, the tone behind the designs shifted away from simple yet playful streetwear and towards a more earnest approach with clear messaging. For example, Stamm's SS25 collection was dedicated to her son, Svante. The show's accompanying press release outlined not only the designer's commitment towards innovation (she proudly boasts about the material she made from 50% banana linen, 50% Japanese paper dyed in charcoal) but also the very human emotion of being worried for the world that the young people of today are walking into. "Since my ambition with STAMM is that it must always be bigger than me, then naturally I hope people will feel something," the designer earnestly wrote in the show notes. STAMM represents a cohort of designers and brands that use their artistic output to send a bigger message to the world while still offering a distinct sense of playful escapism – something that we're all craving.

Stamm's streetwear style takes the runway at the Spring/ Summer 2024 edition of Copenhagen fashion week.

ALECTRA ROTHSCHILD / MASCULINA

After working for the likes of Iris van Herpen and Casey Cadwallader at Mugler before graduating from the Royal Danish Academy in 2022, Alectra Rothschild broke into the Danish fashion scene with her first collection under the name MASCULINA at Copenhagen Fashion Week for the Spring/Summer 2023 season. “It’s not every fashion week that you walk into a show that could easily be confused for a rave,” *Dazed* magazine’s Nicole DeMarco remarked on the designer’s runway debut. In the few short years that MASCULINA has been around, Rothschild’s collections have garnered plenty of attention for taking the notions of high glamour and femininity and flipping them entirely. She told *Vogue* in 2023:

“My clothes have so much to do with the community I’m from – it’s trans people, it’s nightlife people, it’s DJs, it’s musicians ... all these people at the margins of society. I want to put that lifestyle on a pedestal because I think it deserves to be there.”

Alectra Rothschild

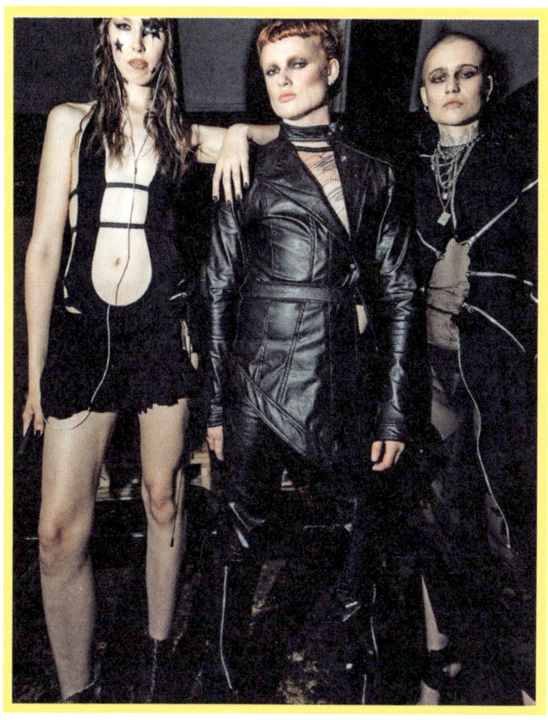

Alectra Rothschild / MASCULINA Spring/Summer 2025 models backstage at Copenhagen Fashion Week.

Dramatic cuts and unexpected materials come alive across MASCULINA collections, paraded around by Rothschild's friends-turned-models, as the designer delivers one of Copenhagen Fashion Week's most talked about shows every season. While Rothschild rejects many concepts typically associated with a Danish designer, she embraces sustainability as a key pillar in her work through the use of zero-waste techniques and upcycled leathers, denim, PVC and deadstock fabrics.

chapter 7

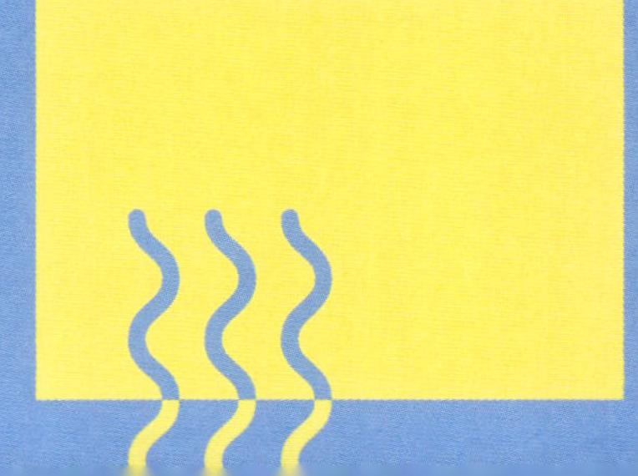

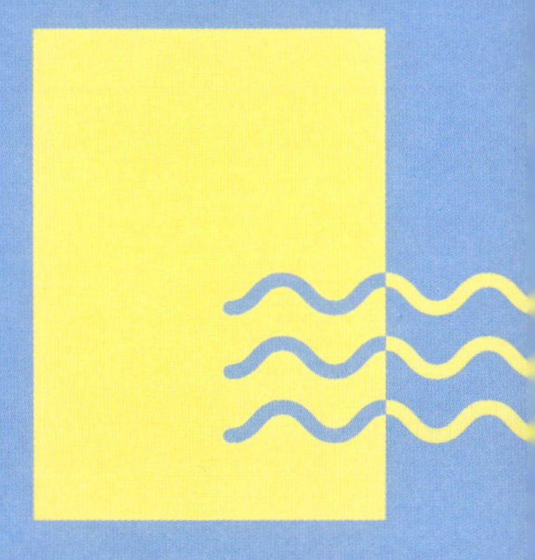

DRESS LIKE A COPENHAGENER

Though the wardrobes of Copenhageners are becoming more varied and diverse, a few essential styles remain that they never stray too far from. With practicality at the forefront for many, dwellers of the Danish capital often rely on a few pillars as the foundation of their sartorial expression.

Staying dry and warm during the colder months could be seen by some as a bother, but residents of one of the happiest nations on Earth see things rather differently. Discover how Copenhagen's best-dressed locals put their own spin on key looks and get an understanding of the connection between the famously leisure-filled lifestyle and the clothing choices they make to match.

KNITWEAR

It wouldn't be an understatement to say that Danes are pretty obsessed with knitwear. It also doesn't take a genius to figure out why. Cold weather is an undeniable reality for Copenhagen residents for much of the year. Pair this with their strong affinity for styles designed with longevity in mind, and knitwear becomes an obvious choice for many Danes.

The roots of Danish knitwear date back as far as there are documented records of the nation's apparel – in short, this obsession isn't anything new but has very much stood the test of time. From the knitted sweaters worn in the nineteenth century to the young Copenhageners using knitting to craft sustainable designs, the craft of knitwear is alive and well in the Nordic capital.

A Copenhagen Fashion Week guests attends the Munthe show wearing a knitted cardigan and scarf in February 2024.

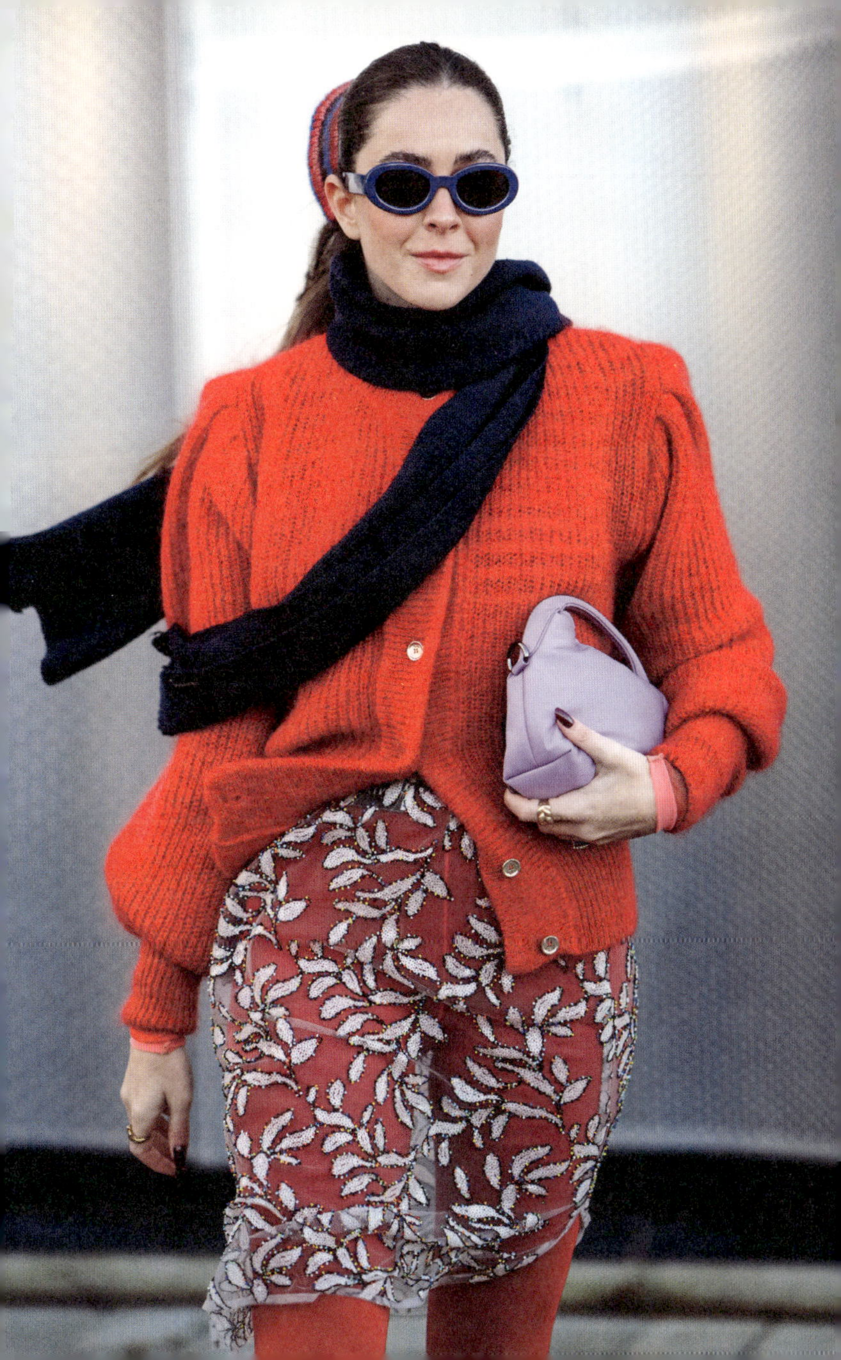

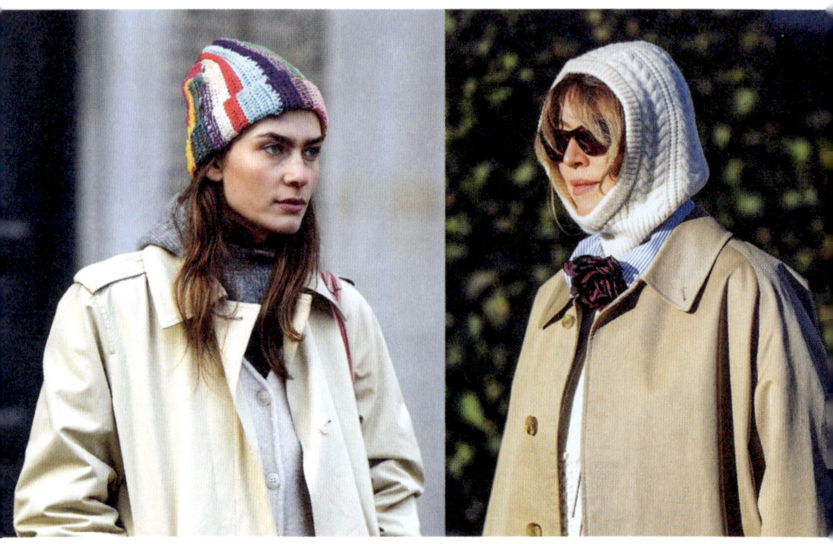

Above left: Beanies act as the ideal canvas for infusing colour into many Copenhageners' winter wardrobes, as demonstrated on a Copenhagen Fashion Week guest in 2023.

Above right: Beyond the beanie, knit hoods like the one seen here on a Copenhagen Fashion Week guest in 2023, are often spotted across the Danish capital.

The beanie (or *hue* in Danish) is definitely a must-have for Copenhageners. Like many of the Copenhagen style staples, the humble beanie is far from just a way to complete a cold-weather outfit. Aside from the obvious added warmth, the beanie is a handy tool for keeping your hair out of your eyes when the Danish wind hits you – which it especially tends to do in the winter months. The added cushioning it provides under your bike helmet doesn't hurt either. Crafty Copenhageners can be seen with their homemade beanies while the signature Mads Nørgaard version can be spotted on the heads of the city's most stylish crowd for many months in a year.

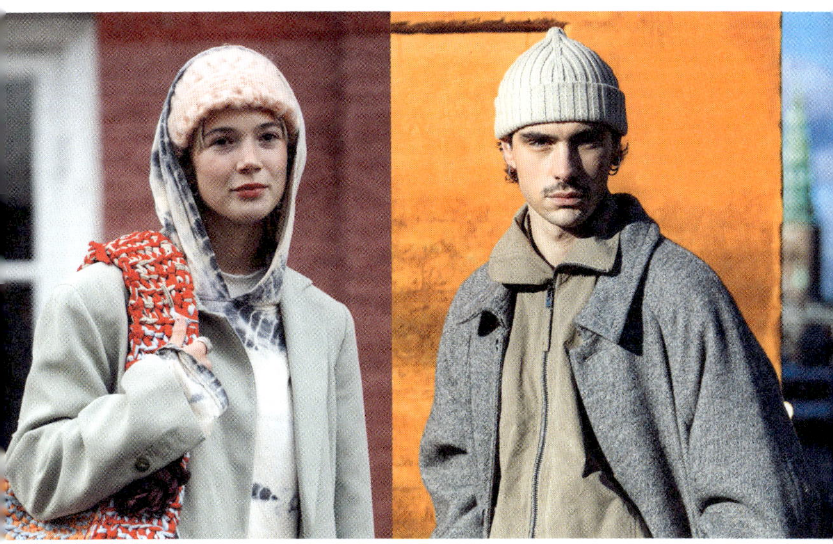

Above left: A Copenhagen Fashion Week guests poses in a beanie and knit bag outside the Baum und Pferdgarten show in August 2023.

Above right: Keeping warm remains a priority for this Copenhagen Fashion Week guest, seen here attending the Autumn/Wintor 2023 edition of the fair.

Labels like Skall Studio and Andersen-Andersen have dedicated much of their output to knitwear styles, the latter referencing traditional Danish knits worn throughout the country's fishing history. On the opposite end of the style spectrum are young designers like Nadia Wire. "Eclectic and colourful, Nadia Wire is the epitome of quirky Copenhagen fashion," expressed *Scandinavian MIND*. So, whichever side of Danish fashion calls to you the most, there are plenty of knitwear options to help you channel your inner Dane – whatever the weather.

HIGHLY FUNCTIONAL FOOTWEAR

"It's no surprise that the stylish, colorful Scandi crowd has a few sartorial rules they live by: Number one, an all-black outfit, though chic, tends to be mundane. Number two is that flat shoes are an essential if you're walking or biking anywhere in the city"

Ana Escalante, *Who What Wear*

By now, you should know how important function is to the residents of Copenhagen when it comes to selecting the best pieces for their wardrobes. Therefore, it should come as no surprise that practical footwear goes beyond a simple sartorial choice – it's basically a religion.

Trainers. Sneakers. Whatever you want to call them, the Danes are frankly obsessed. The Danish style philosophy is all about embracing unexpected pairings, so wearing a trusty pair of trainers alongside a billowing tulle dress is a completely acceptable outfit for Copenhagen's cool girls. Whether worn as part of a laid-back everyday look or for a high-fashion occasion, the Danes always welcome a comfortable pair of

Trainers aren't just for cardio, as proven here in this Copenhagen Fashion Week look from August 2023.

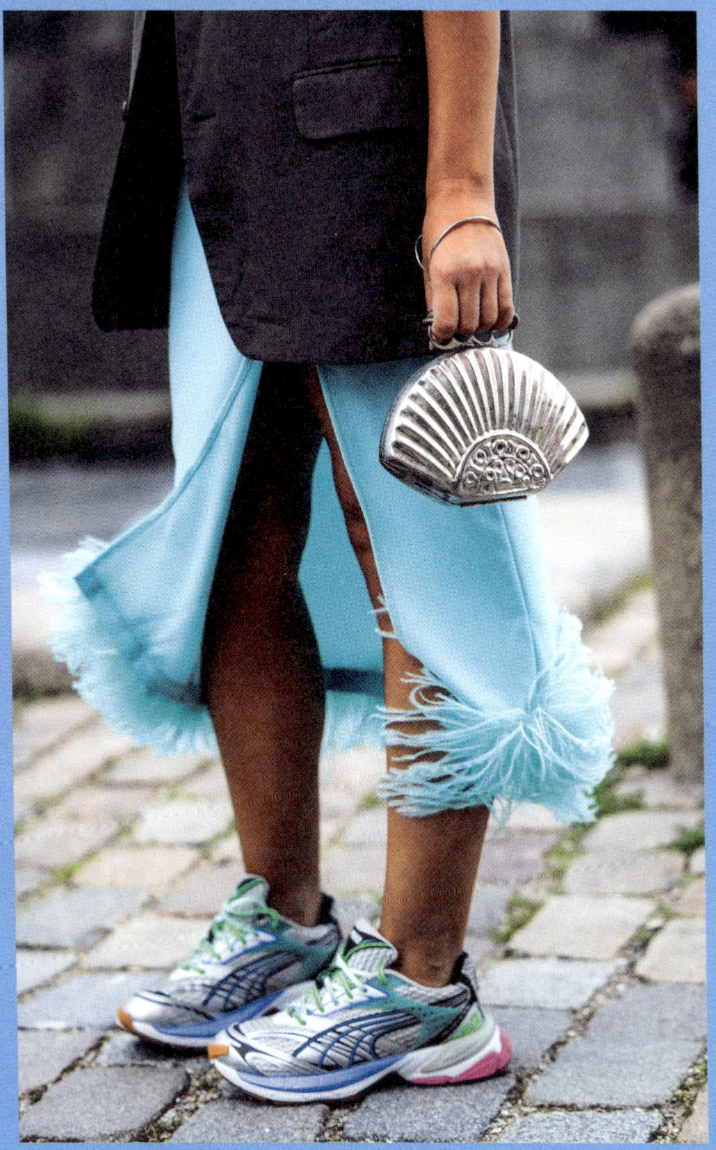

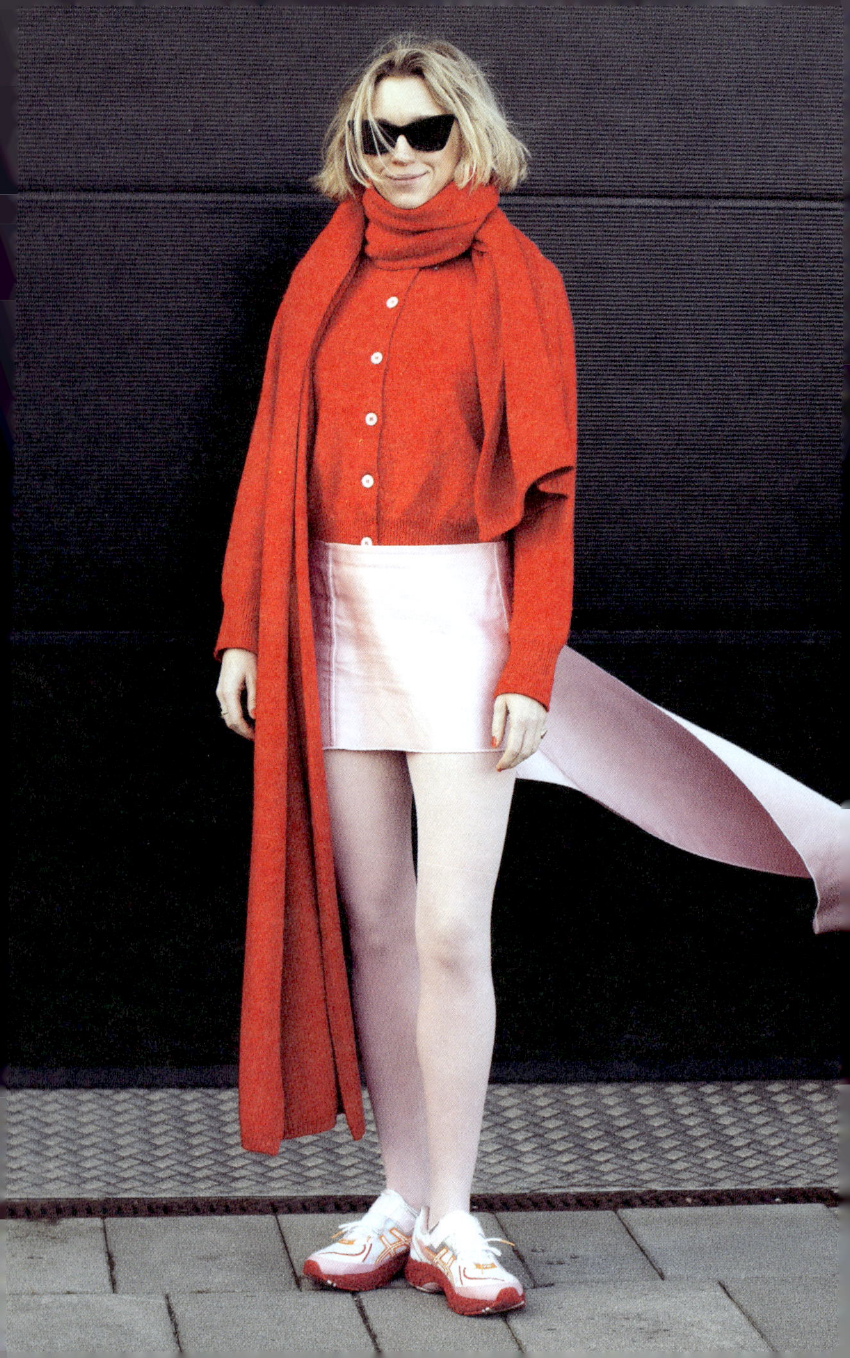

trainers. The active lifestyle that's shared among residents and the rejection of strict dress codes often popular in other European cities makes Copenhagen one of the best places for discovering your next sneaker obsession. While not all trainers are made for running, it's important to note the influence that Copenhagen's thriving running culture has had on the style of many Copenhageners. Brands like SAYSKY and DOXA have emerged out of the country's dedication to embracing an active way of living. Many activewear companies often incorporate the Danish affinity for community into their business outlook, as plenty of run clubs and social events are constantly popping up across the city.

When the weather turns, everyone's second-favourite footwear choice comes out – winter boots. Rather than letting the challenging climate ruin a great outfit, Danes are known to embrace boots in all their chunky glory. While other nations may opt to create streamlined looks with the sleekest footwear options available, choosing to deal with the practical struggles as they come, the quiet confidence that Copenhagen residents embody means that they own their statement winter footwear.

Danish stylist Pernille Rosenkilde, also founder of sustainable label Per and the Zoo, shows off her practical footwear look in February 2024, at Copenhagen Fashion Week.

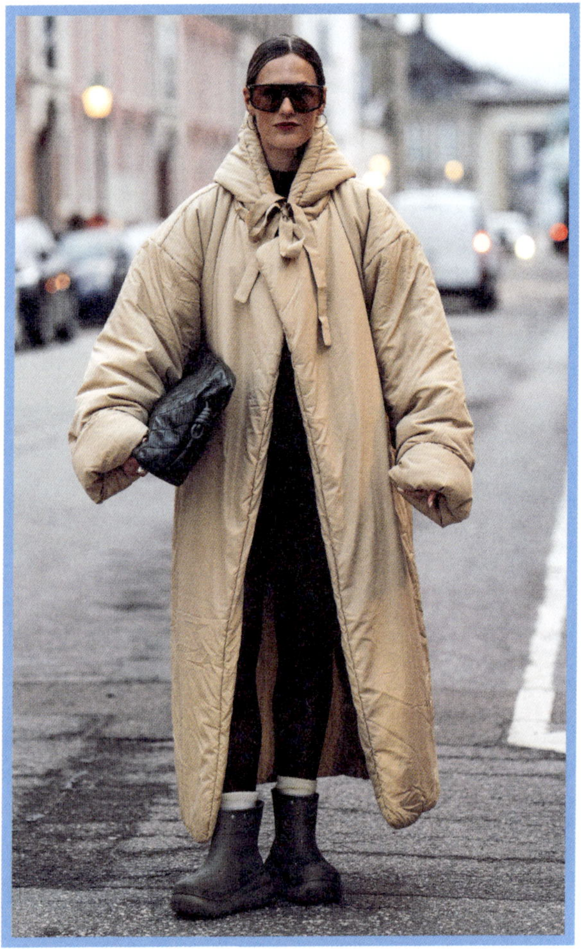

Above: A Copenhagen Fashion Week guest completes their cold-weather ready look with army green boots, pictured here in January 2024.

Opposite: Magasin Du Nord buyer Mike Bjørnbak sports Puma trainers as he takes on the Spring/Summer 2025 edition of Copenhagen Fashion week in August 2024.

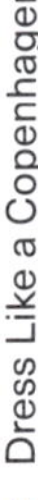

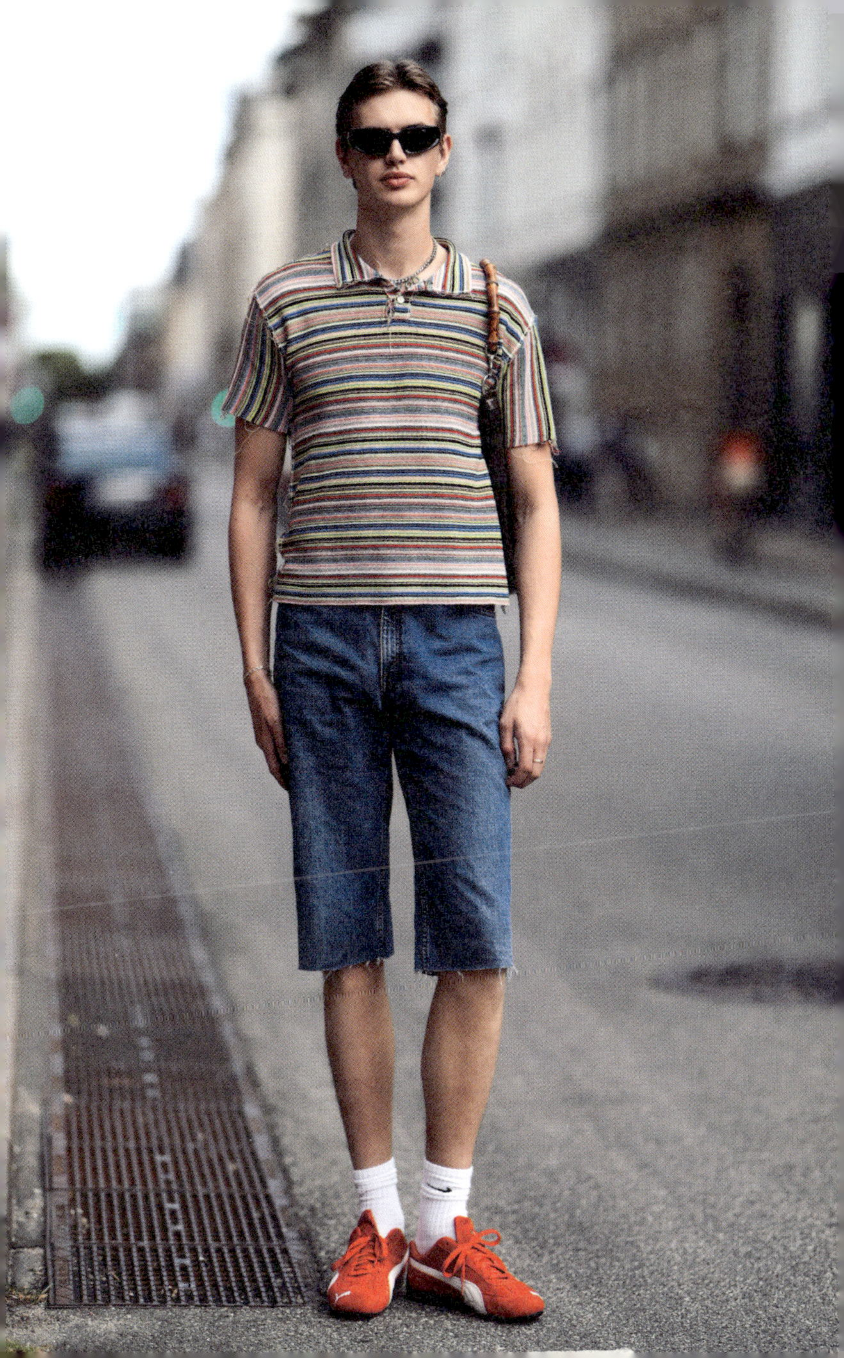

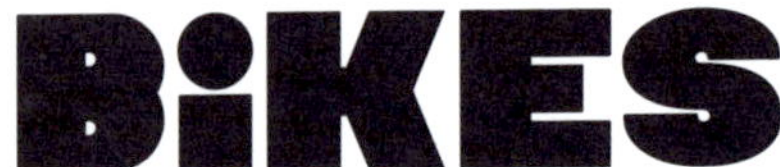

"The city holds a reputation of being the more progressive fashion city in Scandinavia, which also has fostered its own kind of style and aesthetics. Chic but functional, fun but not quirky, elegant but not extravagant – all characteristics that could describe the typical Copenhagen-style, obviously with a bike in hand."

Oliver Dahle, *Scandinavian Mind*, 2022

Throughout this book, there has been a lot of talk about how pivotal bicycles are to Danish culture – so there was no chance of speeding past them here. For Danes, bikes are central to their everyday lives. So much so, that many brands consider how their styles will work while cycling during the design process. Cycling is not only a way for residents to get from A to B but it's also a favoured pastime for many. Pas Normal Studios began in 2013, co-founded by Wood Wood's Karl-Oskar Olsen. Many longtime Wood Wood fans and those looking for a fresh take on the neon Lycra styles that dominated the market at the time were instantly drawn to the label. Now, over ten years later, Pas Normal Studios stands as one of the most recognized cycling labels worldwide.

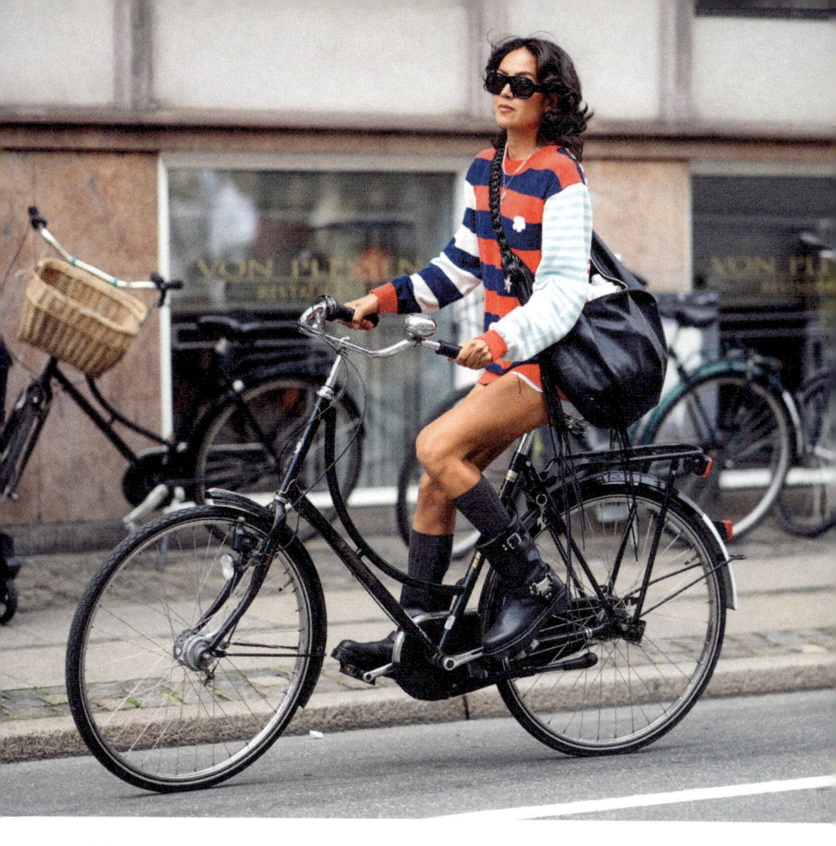

A Copenhagen Fashion Week guest opts for the city's preferred method of transport to get between shows, captured here in August 2024.

For those who prefer a more leisurely approach to cycling, there are plenty of bike rental services available across the city. Each season, Copenhagen Fashion Week inspires countless fashion journalists to publish their own roundups of the most sartorially charged looks sported by attendees with their bikes in tow. This preoccupation isn't lost on the organizers of the event: the SS25 season saw Lime bikes act as an official sponsor to encourage visitors to cycle between the shows.

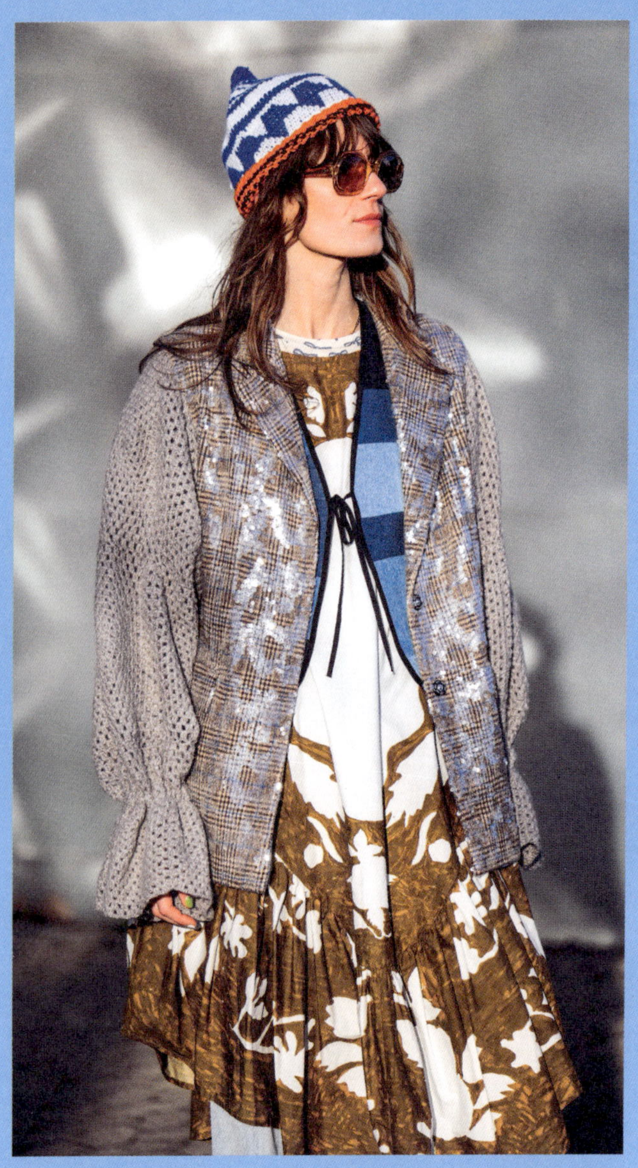

VINTAGE

One of the main ways Danes have created their own distinct style is through their talent for mixing and matching. Most have a knack for pairing contrasting pieces in a way that communicates the region's laid-back approach to life. Unsurprisingly, their love for second-hand and vintage pieces is an essential component for nailing this method of dressing.

Referring to Copenhagen's love for vintage styles, Lilah Ramzi of *Vogue Scandinavia* said: "It's a town of creative innovation and progressiveness, but it's also a place with a great appreciation for history, especially of the sartorial kind." Shopping for unique finds to team with their favourite Danish designer items is a favourite activity for the city's most well-dressed locals – an act that many credit with the formation of "Copencore", an ethos which *Vogue* states "prioritizes practicality" and is "luxurious, yes, but never flashy." In that sense, Copencore's formation can be directly linked to the city's impressive selection of vintage and second-hand clothing shops. Set aside a day to explore these spots and get ready to channel your inner Dane with an ensemble that brings together your beloved styles from the past and present in perfectly imperfect harmony.

A Copenhagen Fashion Week attendee outside a show in February 2023.

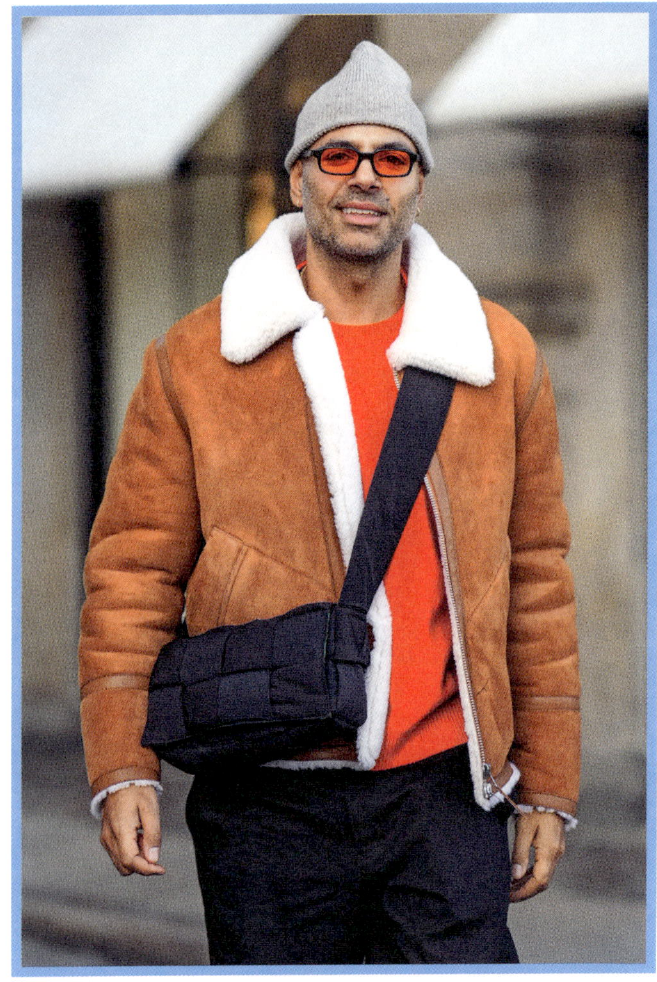

Above: Danish stylist Mads Emil Grove Møller outside Mark Kenly Domino Tan, during Copenhagen Fashion Week Autumn/Winter 2024.

Opposite: Guest outside a Copenhagen Fashion Week show, January 2024.

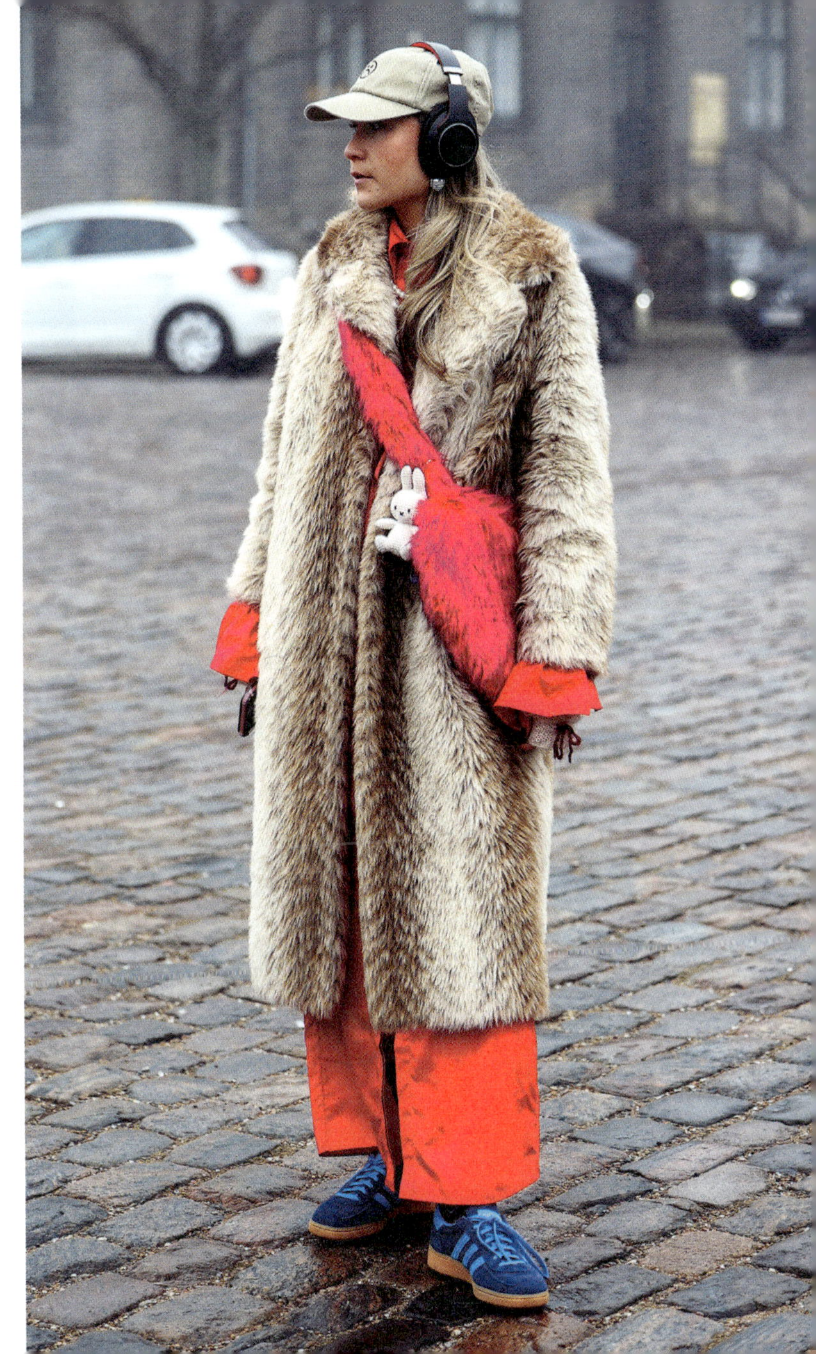

chapter 8

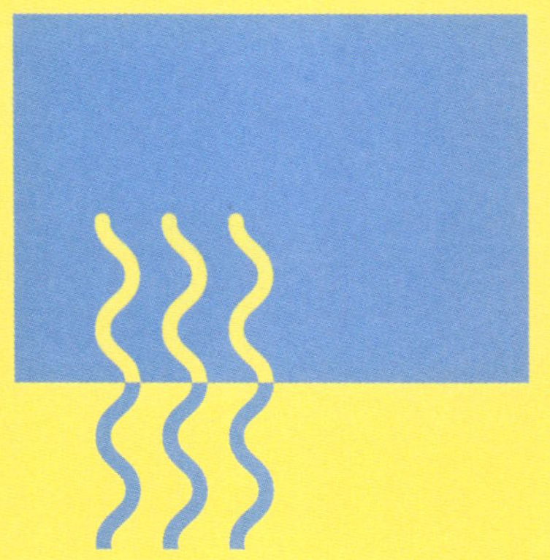

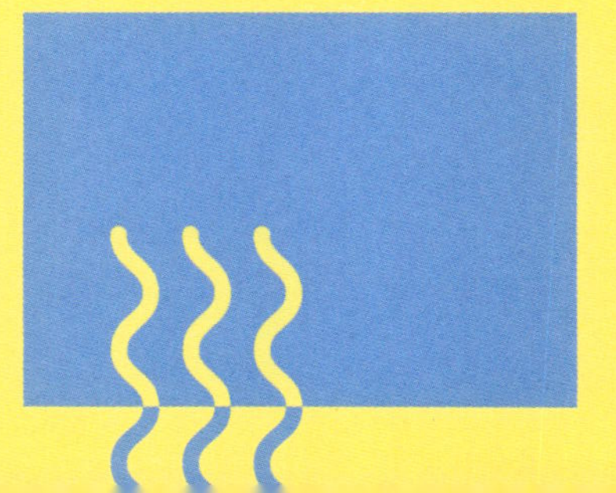

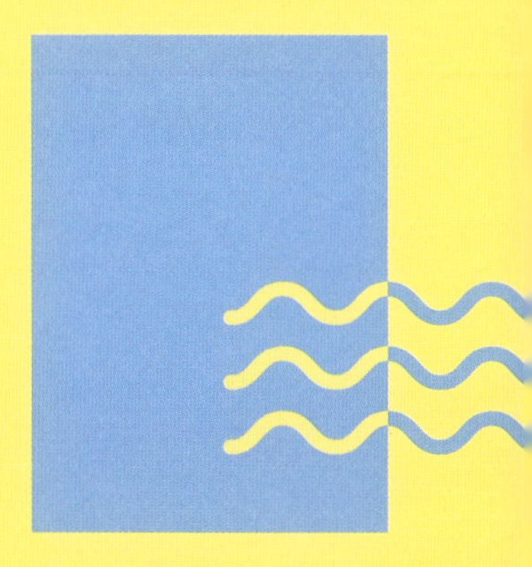

KNOW YOUR NEIGHBOURHOODS

"The best-loved spots around Copenhagen mirror their guests in their aesthetic: they're cool and simple, and the dress code is casual."

Though there are simply not enough pages of this book to outline all of Copenhagen's incredible shopping, cultural or food and drink destinations, in this section we'll outline some of the key spots that haven't been mentioned at length in the previous chapters. Here you'll find a few different places around the Danish capital that are enjoyed by locals and international visitors alike.

VESTERBRO

Starting strong, let's first look at one of Copenhagen's most popular areas for its eclectic mix of restaurants, bars and venues. Vesterbro is home to the city's famous Meatpacking District (Kødbyen) where you can find one of the city's favourite coffee spots, Prolog.

Founded by Sebastian Quistorff in 2016, Prolog was the first coffee bar to pop up in Kødbyen. The spot is known for its inviting atmosphere, premium coffee selection and seriously life-changing ice cream sandwiches – best enjoyed while seated in Prolog's sun-soaked outdoor area. Just around the corner you'll find plenty of options for dinner and drinks, including the famous Kødbyens Fiskebar opened by former Noma sommelier Anders Selmer in 2008. The multi-award-winning restaurant opts for a minimalist approach to decor, with the focus being on serving up fresh seafood dishes with plenty of ingredients that have been locally sourced.

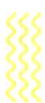

Head down Istegade and you'll find Kyoto, the multibrand fashion destination that houses Danish labels responsible for some of the finest understated styles on the market – discover Colorful Standard, Organic Basics and Rains. Once there, you'll also find some of the country's more fashion-forward labels like Baum und Pferdgarten and Lovechild1979. While at the store, make sure to check out the selection of jewellery from Maria Black: the Irish-Danish designer is a firm favourite among those who like minimalist designs that use earth-friendly materials and practices.

NØRREBRO

If Nørrebro sounds familiar, you may have seen it topping plenty of "The world's coolest neighbourhood" lists over the years (winning first place on *Time Out*'s list in 2021).

Jægersborggade, one of the area's most popular streets, boasts plenty of galleries, boutiques and cafes that are perfect for people-watching. Beer lovers can enjoy some of the city's finest offerings at Brus, which is also home to one of the area's best outdoor seating setups, ideal for summer evenings. Those with an affinity for natural wine will enjoy Pompette, situated on Møllegade, just off the bustling main drag of Nørrebrogade. Pop by apparel retailer Grocery on Elmegade to browse plenty of Danish labels like Palmes, Wette Mille, Another Aspect, Sunflower and mfpen – just to name a few – alongside favourites from abroad. When it comes to cafes, you're spoilt for choice in Nørrebro. Andersen & Maillard does pastries like no one else (the pistachio croissant cubes are life-changing), while Darcy's serves up some of the best coffee around (presented in seriously gorgeous ceramics by local artisan, Marie Lytken).

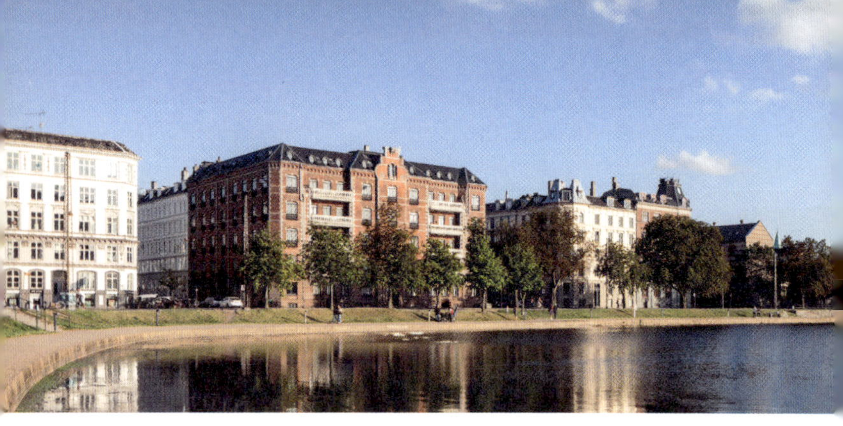

ØSTERBRO

Experience some of Copenhagen's greenest (and bluest) spots in the area of Østerbro. This neighborhood is known for its laid-back feel that attracts plenty of young families for its dreamy swimming spots like picnic-perfect spaces Fælledparken and Sortedam Lake.

Head to the menswear haven that is Goods on Østerbrogade (which stocks a selection of Danish offerings from labels like Andersen-Andersen, Berner Kühl and Norse Projects), or pop next door to experience womenswear brand Stine Goya in all its charm. Just a few metres north on Østerbrogade, you'll come across Dallas, an essential spot for supreme coffee and cakes. Come dinner time, Corsa Pizza promises some of the best the city has to offer. After a short wander around the area, you'll find it's no wonder that Cecilie Bahnsen chose Østerbro for her namesake label's headquarters in 2022.

Above: Sortedam Lake is one of three lakes refered to simply as "Søerne" (the lakes) by locals.

Opposite: One of Frederiksberg's most loved cafes, Hart Bageri.

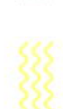

FREDERIKSBERG

More like a city in a city rather than a neighbourhood per se, Frederiksberg is known for its upscale restaurants, designer boutiques and tree-lined streets.

Stroll along Værnedamsvej or Gammel Kongevej and soak in the atmosphere. Get your coffee and pastry fix at the Frederiksberg branch of Hart Bageri, one of Copenhagen's most adored spots for baked goods (hot tip: pre-orders are welcome to avoid disappointment at the front of the queue). Next, head down the road to Mr. Larkin, the iconic womenswear shop home to Danish labels like OpéraSPORT, Saks Potts and THE GARMENT. Looking for a vintage treasure? Paloma Vintage is conveniently located mere minutes away. When you're ready for something stronger, grab a "highball with hi-fidelity" at record store/cocktail bar Bird, known for hosting eclectic DJ sets (expect anything from Brazilian disco to acid jazz – sometimes in one sitting) and signature cocktails made using fresh, seasonal ingredients.

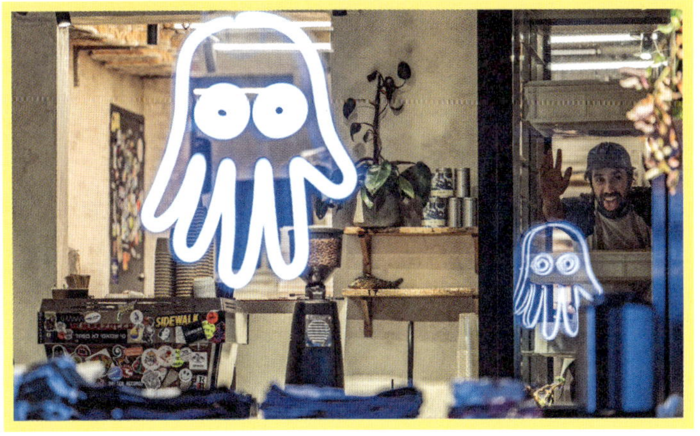

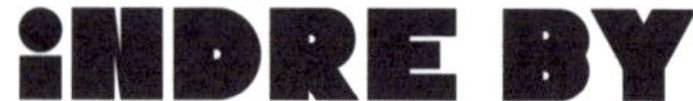

Copenhagen's city centre (known as Indre By) is home to some of the city's most notable spots including the picturesque Nyhavn Harbor, the iconic Tivoli Gardens and the famous Little Mermaid statue.

Around the main shopping streets (Pilestræde and Købmagergade) you'll find shops such as Mads Nørgaard, Stine Goya, Saks Potts, Skall Studios and Caro Editions. This area is also home to a charming little chunk of streets where you can find the flagship locations for five of Denmark's finest outfitters: mfpen, Palmes, Berner Kühl, NN.07 and Another Aspect. Next, stop by one of plenty of the area's cafes for a strong coffee and pastry to keep you going. Atelier September is a popular choice, run by chef Frederik Bille Brahe (the husband of Caroline Bille Brahe, the founder of Caro

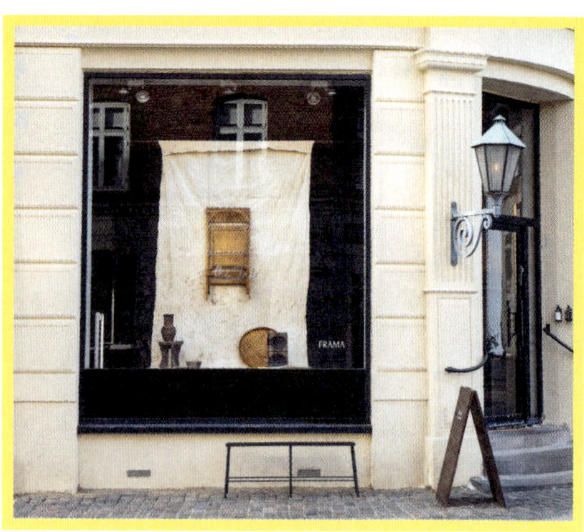

The Frama store building was once home to St. Pauls Apotek and dates back to 1878.

Editions). The cosy spot has become a key player in the city's vegetarian food scene. Another key destination in the area is Apotek 57, a charming cafe situated in the back of Frama, one of the city's most loved homeware shops. Together they attract those looking for both sleek design and fresh eats (presented beautifully, of course). Another one for the homeware lovers is the brick and mortar shop for the bedding masters that are Tekla. The Danish B-corp has been using linens and sleepwear as the foundation for some of the most exciting collaborations since its inception in 2017. Stüssy, Jacquemus, Birkenstock and Artek have all teamed up with the label. Fall in love with the fabrics yourself at Vognmagergade 7.

CHRISTIANSHAVN

Situated just next to the city centre, Christianshavn is a series of islands that makes for a must-visit spot for canal-side strolls and enjoying some of the city's trademark bohemian structures.

The area is home to the famous Freetown Christiania commune neighbourhood which has existed since the 1970s and, though it has experienced plenty of changes over the years, still operates. Head for a plant-based meal at the legendary Morgenstedet, which has been feeding the locals for over two decades, sticking closely to its roots as an independent collective with a passion for organic and fresh ingredients. Familiarize yourself with Copenhagen's thriving contemporary art scene with a visit to Overgaden, renowned for showcasing the works of some of the best up-and-coming artists that Denmark has to offer. And before the sun disappears, cycle up to La Banchina for a dreamy evening of oysters, wine and a quick dip in the water before calling it a day. And I guess a quick sauna couldn't hurt either.

iNDEX

CREDITS

Acielle/Styledumonde.com 118

Alamy: Album 12; Associated Press 41; Marie-Paola Bertrand-Hillion/ ABACAPRESS.COM 83; colaimages 11l, 11r; dpa picture alliance 49; Hemis 33; Thomas Kyn 154; Takimoto Marina/ SOPA Images/Sipa USA 149; Nils Meilvang/Ritzau via AP 82; Moma 9; Vintage Travel and Advertising Archive 24; Mark Waugh 26–27; Zoonar GmbH 107

Courtesy of Caro Editions 100

Courtesy of the Copenhagen International Fashion Fair 59

Courtesy of Frama 157

Getty Images: Martin Sylvest Andersen 110; Rob Ball/WireImage 93; Marcel ter Bekke 55; Edward Berthelot 13, 135, 136tl, 136tr, 145, 148; Yuliya Christensen 77, 78–79, 94l, 94r, 113, 144r; Kuba Dabrowski/WWD/Penske Media 117; DEA / G. Cigolini/De Agostini 29; Stefania M. D'Alessandro 66, 72, 73; Mario De Biasi/Mondadori 36, 37; Estrop 90; Alexander Farnsworth 155; Matt Jelonek 69, 70, 86, 88, 89, 96, 99, 102, 103; Raimonda Kulikauskiene 63, 137tl, 140, 142; Felix Kunze/WireImage 52; Earl Leaf/Michael Ochs Archives 39; Bax Lindhardt/AFP 60; Migeul Medina/AFP 91; Jeremy Moeller 143; Jan Persson 35; Rolls Press/Popperfoto 32; Tim Roney 50, 51; Universal History Archive/Universal Images Group15; Christian Vierig 80, 81, 108, 139, 146; Alexis Waldeck/Conde Nast 42–43; Alena Zakirova/WireImage 84–85, 125, 127, 128; Vittorio Zunino Celotto 74, 97

Magasin du Nord Museum 19, 20-21

Tonya Matyu 131

Courtesy of Mads Nørgaard – Copenhagen 92

Shutterstock: Cynthia Anderson 56; Olga Kuleva 137tr

Skanderborg Historiske Arkiv / Skanderborg Historical Archive 31

Courtesy of Solitude Studios 114l

Courtesy off Time's Up Vintage, Copenhagen 120–121

Vejle Stadsarkiv, Denmark 44; Allan Simonsen 45